SURVIVOR

THE TRIUMPH OF AN ORDINARY MAN IN
THE KHMER ROUGE GENOCIDE

CHUM MEY with Documentation Center of Cambodia
Translation by Sim Sorya and Kimsroy Sokvisal

Chum Mey's confession (with introduction by David Chandler and Youk Chhang)
Documentation Series No.18 - Documentation Center of Cambodia, 2012.

ក្បៀសិង្ហ

Photograph in 1979

Chum Manh
call. Chum Mey   Kuy Nea Kong   Tem Chan   Heng Nath   Bou Meng   Phan Than   Chan Ung Pech

Chum Mey's cell

SURVIVOR

Date....*1.0.*. Month..*1.2.* Year 201....*6*

ជុំ ម៉ី Chum Mey

THE TRIUMPH OF AN ORDINARY MAN IN
THE KHMER ROUGE GENOCIDE

CHUM MEY with Documentation Center of Cambodia
Translation by Sim Sorya and Kimsroy Sokvisal

Chum Mey's confession (with introduction by David Chandler and Youk Chhang)
Documentation Series No. 18 - Documentation Center of Cambodia, 2012.

ស្វែងរកការពិត ដើម្បី ការចងចាំ និង យុត្តិធម៌

Searching for the Truth: Memory & Justice

មជ្ឈមណ្ឌលឯកសារកម្ពុជា

Documentation Center of Cambodia (DC-Cam)
P.O. Box 1110
66 Sihanouk Blvd. Phnom Penh, CAMBODIA
t: +855 (23) 211-875
f: +855 (23) 210-358
e: dccam@online.com.kh
www.dccam.org
www.cambodiatribunal.org
www.cambodiasri.org

SURVIVOR: The Triumph of an Ordinary Man in the Khmer Rouge Genocide
Chum, Mey
Sim, Sorya
Kimsroy, Sokvisal

1. Cambodia—Law—Human Rights
2. Cambodia—History—1975-1979

Funding for this project was generously provided by Friends of the Documentation Center Cambodia with core support from United States Agency for International Development (USAID).

Cover and book concept: Youk Chhang
Graphic design: Yvonne Wong-Fein
Photo credits: Mariko Takayasu and Kimsroy Sokvisal

ISBN: 978-99950-60-24-4

TABLE OF CONTENTS

ACKNOWLEDGEMENTS

This book is dedicated first of all to the souls of my parents, whose memory has sustained me through the hardships of my life. I also dedicate this book to all my fellow prisoners at Tuol Sleng and to all the other millions of people who died during the three years, eight months, and twenty days. And it is dedicated to the generations of Cambodians to come, as a reminder of what can happen, and has happened, in our country: unbelievable horrors committed by their own people that I hope will never be repeated.

I am very grateful to Youk Chhang and the staff of the Documentation Center of Cambodia (DC-Cam) who have worked so hard to preserve the history of the Khmer Rouge years, and who showed such generosity in helping me with this book. In addition I extend my thanks to Sim Sorya Kimsroy Sokvisal and Men Pechet as well as to Seth Mydans and Mariko Takayasu for their kind help with the text.

 **PREFACE**

On April 17, 1975, two weeks before the fall of Saigon in neighboring Viet Nam, the radical communist Khmer Rouge defeated the American-backed army of Cambodian President Lon Nol and marched into Phnom Penh. The last months of the war had seen the Khmer Rouge cordon tighten and the Cambodian capital swelled with refugees and came under heavy artillery bombardment. At the end, almost all foreigners had fled and the Khmer Rouge sealed the country and embarked on a brutal campaign of what might be called social cleansing in an attempt to rid the country of its urban and educated classes and create a pure, self-sufficient peasant society. Within hours of entering the city, the black-clad, often barefoot soldiers began forcing virtually all inhabitants into the countryside in a mass atrocity that cost uncounted lives. By the time the Khmer Rouge were driven from power by a Vietnamese invasion on January 7, 1979, at least 1.7 million people had died of starvation, forced labor and untreated disease as well as torture and execution. The remnants of the Khmer Rouge retreated into the jungles and carried on a guerrilla war that lasted almost two decades.

This book tells the story of Chum Mey, one of only a handful of people who survived incarceration in Tuol Sleng prison, or S-21, a former schoolhouse that became the main interrogation center of the Khmer Rouge. Tuol Sleng is now a museum of genocide, its empty rooms and tiny brick cells still seeming to echo the horror of the past. On its lower floors, thousands of black-and-white portraits line the walls and fill glass panels. They are booking photos of prisoners as they were brought into Tuol Sleng. More than 12,000 of them died under torture or were trucked to a killing field. Very few survived. (An analysis of survivors of Tuol Sleng is appended below.)

Chum Mey then returned to his profession as a mechanic, and in recent years he has focused again on his experiences at Tuol Sleng, telling his story over and over again to journalists and visitors and to anyone else who asks. He has founded a victims association called Ksaem Ksan that accepts donations to help former victims of the Khmer Rouge and seeks to keep alive the memory of their hardships. (Material on Ksaem Ksan is appended below.)

In 2003, the Cambodian government and the United Nations established a joint tribunal to try some of the leaders and major figures of the Khmer Rouge. Chum

Mey has attended many of the court sessions and testified as a witness in the first of the trials, in which the chief of Tuol Sleng Prison, Kaing Guek Eav, known as Duch, was ultimately sentenced to life in prison for crimes against humanity and other crimes. That life sentence, which came on an appeal of a lighter sentence, was a moment of joy unlike anything Chum Mey had experienced in the years since his torture, vindicating his suffering and setting him free, to some degree, from his past. Chum Mey has continued to attend court sessions in the tribunal's second part, in which three top leaders of the Khmer Rouge are on trial. All of them, like Chum Mey, are in their 80s -- among the last survivors a brutal clique -- and as they face each other in the courtroom, this reckoning is a final chapter of closure in all their lives.

This is the third memoir by a survivor of Tuol Sleng and together their stories speak, in a way, for all those fellow prisoners who lost their lives. One memoir is "A Cambodian Prison Portrait, One Year in the Khmer Rouge's S-21" by Vann Nath. The second is "Bou Meng: A Survivor from Khmer Rouge Prison S-21" by Huy Vannak. A thorough introduction to Tuol Sleng is "Voices from S-21: Terror and History in Pol Pot's Secret Prison" by David Chandler. Chum Mey also appears in the documentaries "S-21 The Khmer Rouge Killing Machine" directed by Rithy Panh, and "Behind the walls of S-21: Oral Stories from Tuol Sleng Prison" produced by the Documentation Center of Cambodia (DC-Cam). (A more extensive list of memoirs, histories, films and drama is appended below.)

 # INTRODUCTION

My name is Chum Mey. I am one of only a handful of prisoners who survived Tuol Sleng prison, where more than 12,000 people were tortured and sent to a killing field by the Khmer Rouge regime. I am also one of the last who are still alive today.

For several years, I have been telling the story of my arrest and torture to journalists and other visitors of Tuol Sleng genocide museum and I have testified at the international tribunal that recently convicted the chief of the prison, Kaing Guek Eav, or Duch.

This book is my complete story, the story of a village boy whose only ambition was to be a mechanic and to fix cars and trucks, but who became one of millions of victims of the Khmer Rouge. I survived, but I can't say I was lucky. My wife and children are dead and the torture I endured was horrible. At that time, it would have been better to die than to survive.

But I did survive, and I believe it is my duty to tell my story. If I don't stand up to tell it, the young generation will say 'Chum Mey knew the truth about what happened, but didn't speak out.' I am glad I am here to tell my story. Whenever journalists interview me, I say I don't want to see this terrible time repeated again. I tell that not only to Cambodian people, but to people around the world -- Chinese, Cham [Muslim], anyone who comes to me, so long as I have a translator to pass on my words. I want the world to know what really happened, and I don't want those who died ever to be forgotten.

When I walk among those photographs of the people who died at Tuol Sleng, I see portraits of people who wanted to live. They all wanted to live. Why were they killed? According to Buddhist teachings, those killers will reap their karma. It hurts me to walk among those photos, but I do it in order to tell my story. Sometimes I imagine that I could have been one of those in the photographs who died. It was such a rare chance that I survived when so many people were killed there. I think about it every night, how lucky I was to survive. Why did I survive?

I think maybe in my previous life, I did good things and that's why for this life, I have been spared. Throughout my life, there are 1,000 times I could have died, starting all the way back to 1962 when Khmer Rouge soldiers shot at me. But I have survived. It's something I don't understand. I've been shot at many times and it was close. But I was not killed. Someone else might have been killed. But I survived.

When I was detained in that cell, I did nothing but cry and feel sad and pray to Buddha and my ancestors for help. In Buddhism, there are many lessons for monks, five or ten, that I learned when I was ordained as a monk for a year. When I was there, I was silently saying those prayers. I put my hands together and prayed to my ancestors to help me get out of there. 'Your son did no wrong. Please, father and mother, come and help me.' I couldn't pray aloud or I would have been beaten.

But I do not condemn the people who tortured me. If they were still alive today and if they came to me, would I still be angry with them? No. Because they were not senior leaders and they were doing what they had to do at the time. I consider them victims like me, because they had to follow other people's orders. How can I say I would have behaved differently? Would I have had the strength to refuse to kill, if the penalty was my own death? During the interrogation I was angry, but after a long while, learning about that place, understanding that people had to do what they were told to do, I wasn't angry with them anymore. Even the ones who tortured me, they also lost parents and family members.

There's a saying in the Khmer language: 'If a mad dog bites you, don't bite it back.' If you do, it means you are mad, too.

Chum Mey
July 25, 2012

HIS LIFE STORY

A VILLAGE CHILDHOOD

I was born on a Saturday in November in 1931, the Year of the Monkey, into a middle class family with a house and cattle like other people. I come from Thnaot Chroh village, Lvea commune, Kampong Trabek district, Prey Veng province. All of my relatives lived in Lvea. I did not go to school, but studied in Svay Udom pagoda near my home. My parents passed away when I was a child, just young and naked. In my village people called me Chum Manh, but since I first came to Phnom Penh, I have been called Chum Mey.

I had five brothers and two sisters. My oldest brother was Ka-ek, then my oldest sister It, older brother Yak, older sister Nuon and then my brother Mom and me and then another younger brother named Mai and the youngest one Morn. I ranked number three, counting from the bottom.

My mother helped my father with the farm, together with the older children. We had about two hectares of paddy field and we harvested more than we could eat. We used two pairs of cows to do the farming, and also had several calves.

My father drank wine and after drinking he became a very noisy person, but he never beat any of us children. He just became noisy. He played the Pei- or, a traditional wind instrument for wedding ceremonies, and when I was a boy I went with him. In rural areas, after attending the wedding, guests normally bring cakes home and share them among their children. In the old days, the weddings lasted for three days and nights. When I went with him I would sleep behind him as he played into the night.

One day when I was about 8 or 9, I climbed up onto a tall house that was being built in Boeng Snaor village and fell off the roof and that's why I have this scar on my forehead, until today.

My mother worked in the fields, carrying, transplanting and threshing rice. I was about six years old when she gave birth to my youngest brother. She became ill with postpartum depression, which often happened in the old times. A distant uncle who served as a monk in Svay Udom pagoda and knew about traditional medicine paid us a visit, but he could not save her. After that I lived with my father for about one year until he also passed away, leaving me alone with my brothers and sisters.

LIFE AS AN ORPHAN AT BA PHNOM

When I was about 10, I went to live with my oldest brother, Ka-ek and his family in Ba Phnom. We called the place Chheu Kach mountain. All the rest of my siblings were single at the time except for my oldest sister. I helped my siblings do the farming and find and sell firewood to Chinese businessmen in Prey Veng.

Boeng Snaor village, where I lived, was big, with nearly 100 families. They lived in Thnaot Chroh, Prum Khsach and other communes. In my commune, Kampong Trabek, there were only two families, my aunt's and my mother's. There were three or four families in another village and a family in another village. Most of us were farmers and some earned enough to support themselves while others went to earn money in Phnom Penh and returned home during the rainy season. There was also plenty of fish in a lake and we caught them using Ang-rot, a kind of fish trap in the shape of a basket with a hole at the small end. There were fish, crabs and snails.

FRENCH PERIOD

During the French period, we did not have independence. We often saw the French along the road, although they did not come into the village.

Along the road, there was a French military post that people called Daem Thnaot barrack. It was located in Ta Kok pagoda next to my hometown of Lvea. The French cut down sugar palm trees and used them to make walls and they guarded the road around it using uniformed Khmer soldiers. The French came every day, but they never slept there. The post was guarding against the Issarak but I didn't know what the Issarak wanted. I just heard, 'Issarak, Issarak.' When the Issarak came, the people went along with them. When the French came, they went with the French.

Later, I came to learn that the Issarak were trying to free the country from French rule. Some villagers joined them in this struggle. People helped them, especially at night, and they would punish us if we refused them. Anyway, almost all the people supported the Khmer Issarak.

When the French chased and shot at the Issarak, they fled into the fields. They hid their rifles in the sheaves of rice and pretended to use the sickle to harvest rice like other people until the French soldiers left.

At that time I was 8, 9, or 10 years old. I don't know if my parents or other older people supported them. But the Issarak came and they had rifles. People helped them carry ammunition. For instance, they called my elder brother, Mom, at night to help carry ammunition. He would be back the following morning. As for me, I was too young to understand what they wanted.

I never saw the French arrest a member of the Khmer Issarak. But I did see Khmer shoot Khmer. There were Khmer working at the French military post, and Khmer Issarak would come and shoot at them.

During the day time, the French went and collected taxes in the communes and districts. They taxed everything, including land and houses. I saw this and I heard my father talk about it. I heard people from other districts say the French collected taxes even though people dried their rice on the road in front of their house. When they came to collect taxes, my father and brothers hid in piles of rice and in the pond behind the house.

Sometimes people paid for an official ID card, and sometimes the French soldiers would check the card. My brother Mom fled because he did not pay for his card. You had to have a card to walk freely, and they called it by its French name, Lycée [high school] card. This card had two folds. Another card had five folds, and it was called Ma-Ayos-Mang [lifetime] card. People using this card paid tax only once. For the other card, people paid many times within a year. I don't know how much they had to pay. I heard from my father that people paid tax for farming. We dried rice in front of our house and they collected tax from us. We paid for the land we farmed. I was young and I was not interested in that. I was running around naked during that time.

The Issarak fighters in our area consisted of approximately 6 or 7 people. It has been a long time and they are all dead, and I do not remember their names. I did not know of their weapons, but I was aware there were many of them at that time. The French did not know where they were. They knew they were there somewhere because they fought and searched for them every day, but they did not know their actual whereabouts. Generally speaking, villagers in the whole village helped the Issarak, including my relatives. Like what people said, during nighttime people worked over there, and during daytime, people worked over here. The Issarak did not allow us to raise dogs because they were afraid that they would bark and the French would find out. So all the dogs were killed, wherever they were.

LEARNING TO WRITE

I never went to school at all. There was one layman named Iet, who had just left the monkhood, and had a family. He tended cattle together with me. He asked me whether I wanted to learn the alphabet and I said 'Yes.' So he told me to dry clay collected from riverbank and lake and use it like a blackboard to write on. When the cattle roamed, I went to get them, and after collecting the cattle, I continued my study with him. At that point, I could read a little.

MORE ON FAMILY LIFE

When I was 13 or 14 years old, my oldest brother got smallpox and died, and I stayed with my sister-in-law and her two children. These were difficult years. She had a paddy field and buffaloes, but she did not earn enough to live. When we did dry-season farming, we tried to get water inside the field and tend cattle. We also cut trees to get firewood and brought it home on the backs of buffaloes. We did the same thing every day.

I liked my third brother, Yak, the most. He took after my father, but with darker skin. I took after my grandfather, thin and tall. My mother was short and had light skin. We all dressed the same way, in black trousers and white shirts, which in those days came from France.

All of my brothers liked eating frogs. Normally there were only frogs and eels in rural areas. He loved pork soup cooked with fresh vegetable and any food that drinkers eat. My mother loved ordinary food. She loved A-kaor cakes and Kor-ko soup [Khmer vegetabke soup]. She did not eat much rice. She was really strict and none of us children dared to confront her. When husking the rice, we laid the mat and mortar and if any rice fell out, we had to pick it up, grain by grain.

Usually, I played with my youngest two brothers. My older brothers most of the time just hit me, and we younger brothers could not hit them back. So I didn't like them. We used to hang out and play near the school.

FESTIVALS

We were poor. We didn't even have a bicycle. We had only an ox-drawn Sali cart that we drove for fun. We would drive it during the New Year festival to a pagoda about five kilometers from our house. It's a small cart with a curved body. The ox's tail rose up so we dropped the tail down. We put small bells on their necks. Four people could get into the cart and the oxen pulled it very fast. At one point, during the festival, we went to a village near the Vietnamese border, which was just across a small river. My dad went there to play his traditional instrument and to catch fish. We dried the fish and filled the cart with dried fish.

During the New Year, people took part in boxing, kicking and martial arts contests with a stick. There were many famous experts there. My brother Yak was very good at martial arts and five people could not beat him. He had studied with [Lorkru] Teacher Sum in the village. I used to watch my brother train during the full moon or on festival days. At that time, they did not have boxing gloves. They used bare hands, and there was blood during the fight. They had great techniques, like "lying down tiger." I saw that with my own eyes. They could kick higher than a man's head.

The only other festival was Pchum Ben, the Festival of the Dead, which is one of the biggest Buddhist festivals. And there were also smaller festivals, Baing-skol [praying for the soul] and Bon-phka [flowers festival]. Also there was Ba Phnom, when they killed a person to make an offering to the spirit. That was a long time ago, when my father was young. It could be a man or a woman. People said the sacrificed people were just worthless prisoners. I just heard about that but never saw it. I just saw people making offerings by killing buffaloes.

In some places, there was cock fighting and sometimes horse racing. In Chheu Kach, there was buffalo racing, cow racing, and running that lasted for three days and three nights. There were many games played during the festivals in the olden days. People from my village went to see the festivals and spent the night there. This was because people had nothing to do after the harvesting season. When hearing of any ceremony, they went there.

ORDAINED AS A MONK

When I returned from Ba Phnom, I lived with my brother Yak, who did not have his own family. As soon as I arrived, I was ordained as a monk in Svay Udom pagoda, just for one year, until about 1950. Regulations for adult monks were stricter than for novices. In the mornings, we ate porridge and in the evenings, we drank tea. Both novices and adult monks said prayers, but those of the adults were more difficult. The prayers in Pali tell us not to sin and not to kill people or fish, not to play around and not to threaten our parents. There were a lot of prayers, but I have forgotten them.

After completing my one-year monastic studies, I decided to move on. I received a stipend of 60 riel, a thin, long-sleeved Chinese shirt, Chinese trousers, and a scarf, and I went to Phnom Penh, where I lived in Unalaom pagoda. I had nothing, no watch, no money except for that 60 riel. With 60 riel, I could eat for half a month. I spent my money carefully, just 5 riel for food per day. During the French period the 500-riel note had a picture of a person carrying a watermelon. The color of a 10-riel bill was blue, the 500-riel bill was yellow.

A MOVE TO PHNOM PENH

I didn't know anyone in Phnom Penh, but I had always dreamed of fixing cars since I was a child. Near my house there were cars along the road, although my house was a bit far from the road. I used to watch the cars, and I made cars from clay and played with them with other kids. Before I left my village, I had never touched a car or been inside of a car. I had only seen them passing by. When I arrived in Phnom Penh in 1950 or 1951, I looked for a job as a taxi driver's assistant, changing the oil and putting air into the car tires. At that time, I had nothing else to do.

I had nowhere to sleep in Phnom Penh and just covered my face with my scarf to keep the dogs from biting me. I slept under a roof in front of a Chinese merchant's house in Dararith park, next to the Unalaom pagoda past Preah Anlong. Soon I ran out of money. I didn't know what to do with no money to buy food or pay for transport back home. It was really difficult to find work because I knew no one there. I was completely poor. This is the way it was for half a month. When I saw soldiers walking past, I told them that I wanted to be a soldier. But they said they are not taking in any new recruits.

Then a Vietnamese guy carrying rope approached me on the road near Kandal market. There was a boat going Roka-kong and he asked me whether I wanted a job. He did not speak Khmer clearly. I asked him what kind of job? He said, carrying firewood. I asked him where. At Prek Ta-it in Kampong Cham, he said. He said he would pay me 300 riel and I was thrilled. I told myself that 'Now, I have a job!' I thought that even 100 riel would be enough because I had no money at all. Then I helped him carry the rope to his boat and I took the boat to Roka-kong here was another person named Him, who was well-built and had dark skin, and was hired to work in the boat. So there were two of us. The boat owner had two boats and his father had one, so there were 3 boats in total. We rowed the boat to Kampong Cham, as there were no motors. The wife rowed the boat, and so did the husband. Him also rowed the boat. And I also rowed the boat. Everyone rowed the boat, so I had to learn to do it like the others. One day, after working too hard at the oars I became numb and I fell overboard. The rowing was very difficult, so they rented another boat to pull our boats to Prek Ta-it. When we reached Tik Thnal, the water was flowing quite strong. We carried the firewood onto the boats and sold it at Roka-kong.

One night the water was flowing very strongly and the boats were separated when the rope broke. The owner's younger sister and father called me, 'Roeun! Roeun! Help! My brother's boat has been separated!' At that time, my name was Roeun. We hadn't gone to bed yet. Him was smoking narcotics, and I had learned to smoke narcotics as well. But when I smoked it, I choked and got a headache and threw up. Him was lazy and pretended to fall asleep, so I ran along the riverbank with the woman to catch the boat. Her brother threw the rope to me, and I tied it to a big dead tree. I was tying the rope with the tree and I had no idea that I was tying that woman to the tree as well. She shouted, and I got the rope untied in time, but she had a big scrape on her thigh.

The next morning I decided to leave. When we arrived in Roka-kong, we got the firewood off the boat. But instead of helping, Him stayed onshore and drank at Roka-kong together with the police under a Kra-khop tree. I went and called him, but he did not want to leave, so I pulled him and he walked back slowly down the road. Two Chinese children were riding a bicycle down the road and almost hit him. He could have fallen into a big hole filled with foul, stagnant water. Finally, we got him sober and back onto the boat. I had already gotten all the firewood onto the shore and decided not to travel with them anymore because Him was not going. He had run off back to Phnom Penh, without even picking up his salary.

I thought, 'I don't want to work like this anymore.' I was doing all the work myself and the working conditions were tough. We ate three meals a day, but always the same thing, fuzzy melon soup with chicken. Nothing changed. So I said goodbye to my boss, telling him I was going to visit my home for a month. He said a month is too long, I should just go for two or three days. So, I just picked up my salary and left.

When I got home I bought a bicycle for 30 or 40 riel. My brother was thrilled to see me. I had left without telling him goodbye and he had no idea where I was. But he went to a spiritual teacher who told him I would not die because someone was watching over me.

It was the summer of 1951. My sister-in-law asked me not to leave again. My brother already had a family and I could not stay there. But I wanted to fix cars, so I returned to Phnom Penh. I found a place to live at Phsar Tauch market, near a riverbank. It isn't there anymore.

FINDING NEW JOBS

One evening I saw a thin old Vietnamese man driving a truck near Phsar Tauch. In those days, trucks used for carrying soil were called fako and they ran on gasoline, not diesel. The elderly man was working alone, without a driver's assistant. Next morning, I went and looked for him, and I saw him changing the truck's water and oil. I went up to him and asked him to let me work as his assistant. He looked me up and down and said, 'Come with me.' So I joined him in his truck. I didn't get a salary. He just let me live with him and he gave me some money. His name was Kim. We transported soil from Russei Keo to Phsar Tauch, back and forth. In the morning he ordered me to check the truck's oil. He told me to start the engine and he looked at the gears to make sure everything was properly engaged. He taught me how to use the gear shift, from neutral to first to second to third gear. In the morning I would start the engine for him. For about two months we worked transporting earth to Sne dam from Prey Veng, near my home village.

Two months later, he returned home. His house was located near Phsar Tauch market where he lived with his wife. Both of them were elderly so I helped wash their clothes and carry water and chop firewood. Their house was located right at Phsar Tauch market where there used to be a big hospital. I lived with them for about a year before they returned to Viet Nam in 1952. He was not born here, and he could not speak Khmer clearly. His children probably called him to come home. After he left, the state took the truck back and hired another driver. He asked me not to go and he gave me work with his friend fixing machines in a state garage Pliti [in French], that was located in front of the big hospital.

I studied mechanics there for about a year until 1953 and learned all the parts of the machines and how to take them apart. I passed an exam and I asked to be assigned to Prey Veng, because it was next to my home village. At Prey Veng, I worked for two or three years for the state public works office as a mechanic fixing cars. I waited in my workshop and fixed any cars that came in with problems.

LIFE IN PREY VENG AND RATANAK KIRI

In 1954, when we gained independence, I was studying mechanics in Phnom Penh and I saw the parliamentary election. After that I worked for about four or five years in Prey Veng until I was transferred to Lumphat provincial town in Ratanak Kiri province in 1960.

People in Prey Veng did dry-season farming and caught birds, which mostly arrived just before Khmer New Year. Prey Veng birds. Delicious! While I was in Prey Veng, the Viet Cong were fighting the South Vietnamese troops. I had never heard of the Viet Cong, but they gave out leaflets that said, 'Support the Viet Cong.' We had no conflict with the Viet Cong, but they laid mines in our country. People were demanding independence and there was military training nationwide, both men and women, training with wooden rifles made from Kapok trees, to help bring independence. People guarded our workplace at night, but I did not know how to fire a rifle.

Most of the vehicles I fixed carried rock for road construction. There were Russian and Chinese and American and French cars. I also fixed tractors and motor graders and rollers and all sorts of construction equipment. They were paving over old ox-cart trails and turning them into roads that ran to the Vietnamese border. I worked there until 1970 and became the chief of about 20 mechanics. I earned 3,000 riel and received another 3,000 riel from American aid. Back then that was a lot of money and I was quite rich.

The area was very developed, with a market called Lumphat and eight or nine schools. There were daily workers who cleared away trees to make way for the road. Most of the people there picked climbing plants to make a living. They were slash and burn farmers. They dug a small hole and put two or three grains of rice into it. They ate loofah and fuzzy melons. They weren't real Khmers. They were mostly ethnic minority groups, like Kuoy and Khmer Leu. There were also Kola, Ta Kuon, Ta De at Lumphat, all in different villages speaking different languages. They mined for gems in Bar-keo and went back and forth to Lumphat to buy goods and do business. There were also Lao people who farmed there and spoke Lao. Their families had come to Cambodia to live a long time ago and they were born here. They formed the majority of people in Lumphat, followed by Khmer Leu. Their traditions and festivals were similar and they drank jar wine and danced together. So we mixed.

During their funerals they took a tree with a hole in it, polished it and used it to cover the body, which they put in a jar. Like Khmer people, they had plates, pots and spoons buried with the body. They put all those things in the jar and then buried the tree, the jar and the body, usually lying down. After that they played music and danced and sang happily. They didn't cry. We had fun during the night. Everyone had to drink, that was the custom. They drank together using ten straws and if we didn't drink they would say we didn't like them and didn't like their wine.

From what I knew, there were about 30,000 people living in Ratanak Kiri province. In Lumphat, there were mostly Khmer. Other groups didn't live there and stayed in their villages in the forest. They just came into town to do business and sell their goods. In those days people traveled by cart and bicycle. Big shots rode in cars. I never saw any Americans there, but the Americans paid for our work.

At the workshop, it seemed there was no boss because he never came and paid me a visit. I was in charge of everything, along with another deputy chief. Sometimes I worked in the workshop and sometimes went out to supervise the road building, maybe four times a month for two or three days at a time.

THE WAR ARRIVES

In 1969 and 1970, chaos erupted between the Khmer Rouge and the Lon Nol government. We ended up working in Pol Pot's territory in 1970. So when we built a bridge, they burned it. And we went to build the bridge again and they burned it again. Soldiers shot at me, four or five times a day. If we had gotten into a small river, we would have been trapped. We walked very carefully, looking down to avoid booby traps with pointed sticks that could slice into your body. The traps were strong enough to catch an elephant. They had something like a crossbow inside that fired arrows at us with poison tips. One time our captain was hit and we couldn't pull the arrow out. We had to break its tail and then pull it out. That happened near my workplace at Traveaux, about two kilometers from the provincial town. Luckily the captain survived.

There was a mountain there called O Ya-da, and when we climbed it we could see American planes. They called the planes to land on a field, known as Plai-kou. It was very cold up there on the mountain and there was no sunlight. There were Lon Nol soldiers and police in the area and they were under strict orders not to mistreat the ethnic people. If they mistreated them or harmed their daughters, the provincial governor would arrest and imprison them.

There was a river in the forest where the people caught fish and it never ran dry.

Their dry season is different from ours. It could be dangerous to be in the water because it could rise very fast. When we heard snails making a sound we knew we had to get out of the water very fast and climb a tree because an enormous amount of water would come gushing at us. Then the next day it would disappear.

The scar here on my head is from a stone that hit me when a tractor got stuck in the sand of a small lake. We went with a truck to pull it out, and suddenly the tractor disappeared for no reason. It just sank and disappeared. When I dived down to find the tractor I hit my head on a rock.

I never had a problem with my co-workers or superiors. Wherever I went everything was fine. If someone said something harsh to me I just walked away and shed a tear. During those years people never had any problems with local authorities or with local villagers. We were free to build roads anywhere. Farmers only worked their land for a year in any one place before moving on. They were slash and burn farmers. They weren't educated. They didn't know their own ages. They didn't know how long they had been farming.

ENTER THE KHMER ROUGE

The Khmer Rouge emerged at Lumphat and Ratanak Kiri in 1967 or 1968. They would surround and attack police posts. I never saw the actual fighting, but I saw one police post that had burned down. No one died when they burned the police post, but the fire spread to the forest and everybody fled. Most of the police there were older and came from far away, mostly from Takeo province. Teachers came too and one was killed. He was captured while out hunting in the forest. He was a relative of the provincial governor, Ung Nhach. The Khmer Rouge hated anyone related to the governor. So they killed him. But they would not kill ordinary people. We were doing construction along Bar-keo Road, clearing the forest with a bulldozerin order to transport government soldiers. Without a road for transporting goods, we had no food to eat in Ta-veng. We ate just one meal a day in an armored vehicle. We made coffee with palm sugar. People often got really bad diarrhea sitting in the armored vehicle. Sometime in 1968 I went with the soldiers in a group of three people. The Khmer Rouge surrounded us and we could not escape. So the road builders had to help rescue us while the soldiers guarded us. The bulldozers cut a road for an armored vehicle to come rescue us.

Now with the Khmer Rouge controlling the area of Ta-veng, we collected all of our people and moved into the towns, some into Banlung, some into Bar-keo and some into Lumphat. This happened between 1968 and 1969.

I didn't know anything about the Khmer Rouge movement. I just knew about it when they shot at me. The worst attack came in a village called Chen Chanh. Later, Bar-keo was also hit hard. They tried to attack us, but they attacked the wrong place. After 1970, I could not stay there anymore because the king had been overthrown and the Pol Pot forces took control of Mondul Kiri. After Mondul Kiri, they got Kratie. So they cut our road, and we had no road to travel because everywhere else was forest. They also took control of Stung Treng province. So only Ratanakiri was left.

They attacked every two days. One time at night, they ambushed and took control of the police station's telecommunication system. Several soldiers were killed and the government sent in a DAKOTA plane from Phnom Penh. There was no way for people to communicate with the plane because the police station had been destroyed. So one captain said, 'Mey, what should we do? The landing area was surrounded by Khmer Rouge and if the plane landed they would shoot at it.' He told me to get the logging truck and park it in the middle of the field. I drove to Lumphat field, left it and ran for my life. The Khmer Rouge were chasing me and shooting at me. I ran from Lumphat lake to the market, and then to the transportation section, where the workers there had no idea what was going on. But it worked. Seeing the truck in the middle of the field, the plane did not dare to land. Instead, it land Banlung, where people had walkie-talkies and could communicate with it. The people on the plane told us the police station might be attacked at night and ordered us to transport people from Lumphat to Banlung by truck. At 8 am, we collected and transported people and they couldn't bring with them anything, but the clothes on their backs.

The Khmer Rouge continued their attack on the telecommunication system and burned that place down. We heard gunshots throughout the morning, and it was reported that we lost the trucks at O-kan. There were five trucks coming to take villagers. They killed all the drivers and burned all the trucks, right there where the plane had wanted to land.

After the trucks were burned, we had more trucks, about 25 altogether, and we used them all to collect and transport people. The soldiers collected soldiers. We were helping each other. At approximately 12 am, we left. They shot at the helicopter that was escorting us and they were shooting at us and blocking us from moving further. Some of the people in the truck became terrified and took their children and jumped out. Some escaped along the forest, some along the lake.

I was not a soldier, but the soldiers gave me a rifle and two magazines. At that time, everyone was fleeing to survive. I got in a truck together with the driver and there was one person hiding right next to it. The Khmer Rouge blocked us and began shooting at my truck so we turned around and drove to the base of a nearby khlong tree and jumped off like green frogs and escaped. They had shot and destroyed our walkie-talkie, so I told everyone to head back to BanLung, which was still safe, with lots of soldiers. The fighting lasted for another night and the Khmer Rouge attacked the transportation section. We dug trenches and lots of ammunition was used that night. The fighting ended at 5 am and about 40 Khmer Rouge soldiers were killed.

Lots of people wanted to leave. I had a mission letter and I got permission from the deputy governor to board an American plane and return home. That was in July or August. A month after I arrived in Phnom Penh I heard that they had taken over BanLung, and even controlled the road from Bar-keo to Plai-kou, Viet Nam.

MARRIAGE

When I was 33, I got married. I was in Ratanak Kiri at that time and my unit chief, Chip Chheng Bun, arranged a marriage with his cousin. I had met her once before in Ratanak Kiri when Chip Chheng Bun's mother asked me how much money I had. I was single and had saved up some money, given that I was earning 6,000 riel a month. His mother arranged everything for the bride's family, including dowry. I paid a lot, 10,000 riel in gold. From my family, my brothers and sisters and two cousins came to the wedding. Unfortunately, I don't have any photographs of the wedding because we buried them at a pagoda when Pol Pot took over. There is nothing left. We didn't dare to keep anything. And now all my relatives are gone. Not one is still alive. The wedding took place in Kampong Chhnang, where my wife lived, and after we married I was given a leave to stay there with her for one month.

Her name was Sam Savorn and she was perfect. She never confronted me. She never spoke out loud to me at home. Unfortunately her father had died and she was an orphan. She and her sister lived with her mother. She was Khmer but she could speak many languages: Chinese, Vietnamese and Cham [Muslim]. She was really smart. As for her appearance, she was fairly dark, thin, and she walked with a stoop. She had a scar on the right side of her forehead that came from being cut with bamboo during a child's game. I was very happy with her.

Knowing that she could speak 3 languages, I thought she would do well at business and later I learned she was really good at it. After we got married, I still worked in Ratanak Kiri and she stayed in Kampong Chhnang selling groceries in her house. I visited often by plane during work trips to buy equipment like spare parts for trucks and tractors. I would usually stay two or three nights. I just told the pilots I needed to go and they would take me.

CHILDREN

During our life together, we had four children. The first two were daughters, Chum Sopheap and Chum Kanady, both of whom disappeared during the Pol Pot time. I don't know what happened to them. I learned after 1979 that both my daughters were taken to Pursat or Battambang province by train, but I'm not sure. I heard there was a train explosion later. I think they both died because if they had survived, especially the first daughter, who was 13 at the time, they would have heard my name for sure. Even if they were were abroad. I have traveled to lots of places, Asia, Europe, America, so they must have heard of my name if they were still alive. I have searched for them for a long time, but never heard any more news of them.

We had two sons. The first, Chum Phalla, died at the age of 3 at Chraing Chamres during the evacuation from Phnom Penh. The second son was born while I was in Tuol Sleng prison and was two months old when he died.

In 1970, I took my wife with me to live in Phnom Penh, probably in July or August. I went to work for the transportation department and lived in Tuol Kauk, east of the Military Police School. My workplace was located to the south of Wat Phnom, which is where the Ministry of Transportation is now. We had responsibility for the whole country. No matter what province, like Prey Veng, Svay Rieng, Battambang, or Kampong Cham province, when they needed mechanics for repairing trucks or tractors, they came and contacted us. So all the ministry cars that went on field trips had to be fixed there. Almost 100 people worked there and I was group chief for eight people. We divided up the work among the groups.

In Phnom Penh, I took a big cut in my salary, down to 3,000 riel from 6,000 riel in Ratanakiri. I was told the Americans had cut off aid. My shift was from 7 am to 1 pm. I did not work in the afternoon. My wife and I lived with one of her relatives who sold vegetables in the market.

In 1972, I opened my own garage. At that time there were no Vietnamese living in that area. The garage was near Santhor Mok school and I called it Thma Da. I had eight workers and lots of customers and we couldn't keep up with the work. So after four or five months, I opened a second garage, also employing eight people, called Stat [Stadium] garage near Olympic Stadium. Our income rose gradually, but at the same time, the riel was losing value. After about a year, two French guys saw we were doing a good business and wanted to join us. One of them was half-French and half-North Vietnamese. He was also a mechanic. They had skills we needed, like making keys or using certain tools, and they got one-third of the profits. They stayed with me until Chan Reangsey called me to fix tractors because he was fortifying his bases along National Road 4 to defend against the Khmer Rouge. The French guys only knew how to fix cars.

WORKING FOR A GENERAL

The Ministry of Transportation asked me to work for Chan Reangsey, an uncle of Sihanouk. He was a brigadier general in charge of all the zones along Route 4. He used a helicopter and a jeep with a gas container on the back. People from the ministry came to me three times and when I refused, they kept coming back and asking me to help. 'Younger brother, he needs your help and it's not good to tell him no. Just go.'

So I sold my garages and went to work for him. I sold the garage located on the right-hand side of the stadium for 250,000 riel, and 200,000 riel for the garage at Santhor Mok. I sold everything and I went to them with empty hands. From then on I worked for Chan Reangsey as chief mechanic fixing cars and tractors until Kampong Speu was liberated.

Chan Reangsey was over 50, short and well-built with a big face and bald head and he had his own way of speaking. He was also a prince, but he was bigger than the king. His mouth was bigger than the king's, but still he looked quite similar. He didn't carry a gun, but a whip. He was firm with his troops, but not harsh. He never had any money with him. His soldiers, captain and major, kept the money. When people got hit by a car, he would take them to a hospital in his own car and give them money. I heard this from others. I never saw it happen with my own eyes.

I often went around with him. He talked with me about work. Sometimes a lieutenant colonel or a colonel dared not go see him, but I could go meet him in person. I didn't have a uniform or a rank. I was just an ordinary citizen, a civil servant, not a soldier. But you could see he liked me. Sometimes he gave me money and when he needed me, he had a major or lieutenant come to call me, not a private.

At that time, I was head of Public Works in Kampong Seila sub-district of Kampong Speu. I reported directly to Mey Ly Seng, supervising more than 30 people in a workshop but I had a direct connection with Chan Reangsey. I stayed in that position until Liberation Day.

THE WAR INTENSIFIES

During this time, my wife was living in Tuol Kauk with her relatives. In the evening, I took a motorbike, a VESPA, home. In the morning, I drove to work. The war was all around and I witnessed some incidents. Sometimes I saw wounded Lon Nol soldiers. They were firing their artillery and I had to crawl and lie down like many others. This kind of thing took place a lot near Kraing Sambo lake. They fought each other hard, chasing and shooting. At that time, everything was in chaos. The Khmer Rouge attacked every night. People fled to safety with us.

I remember one day in 1973. I couldn't get to work because the Khmer Rouge had ambushed and blocked the road. At about 9 am, I saw the soldiers capture some Khmer Rouge and put them inside a tank. They put one Khmer Rouge whose leg was broken into the back. I don't know how long he had been beaten. Then I went ahead to work. I don't know where they took the Khmer Rouge.

In Svay Kravann, the Khmer Rouge ambushed and burned a military base. A number of the soldiers' family members were killed and the houses of civilians were burned down. I saw badly burned bodies in the houses. I heard about this attack when I was driving my VESPA to work. People told me the Khmer Rouge had attacked because refugees had gathered and settled down there. After that I went and saw the site. I saw people who had been terribly burned, and there were 5 or 6 bodies. Some were crying and some were shouting. Things were safe in the daytime, but not at night. That was in 1973 and the Khmer Rouge almost took complete control of Kampong Speu.

I had relatives in Svay Rieng, but there was no way to get news of them. Prey Veng was also taken over by the Khmer Rouge. The area was being bombed and it was impossible to cross the river, so all connections were cut. There was also no connection with Kampong Chhnang and no news from my wife's mother and relatives. The Khmer Rouge kept advancing closer and closer, and they were mistreating people, and more and more people fled toward Phnom Penh. But once they were evacuated, it would not be easy for them to return. That went on for about two years, from 1973 until just before Pol Pot entered Phnom Penh in 1975.

I stayed in that job until one day in 1974 – I don't remember the day – the Khmer Rouge were surrounding Kampong Speu and at about 1 pm, we abandoned the workshop. Some of the workers were forced to join the Khmer Rouge, but those who could escape went to Phnom Penh. Chan Reangsey told his subordinate to take me back by helicopter. I was taken to a place where he was staying, near an intersection of the roads leading to Kampot and to Kampong Som, down near where the railroad crossed the national highway. It was the home of Prince Samanmeth, and Chan Reangsey had made it his headquarters with helicopters and tanks stationed there. Chan Reangsey met me and said, 'Brother, go home. If I need you I'll have someone go and call you.' Then he had a driver take me home, near the front of the policy military school. All this time the Khmer Rouge were firing their artillery from Baset mountain to Phnom Penh, aiming at military camps. Chan Reangsey had told me he would call me when peace returned, but peace didn't come. In fact everything became more chaotic and tense.

We had to keep on working and we sold vegetables at the market as usual. I had sold my garages so I could only work for the transportation ministry with a small salary. But inflation was really high and the currency became very weak. People kept going to work at the ministry but only in the morning. Everyone stopped working at 1 pm. In 1974, we could not travel along the highways and so the only way in and out of the city was by helicopter. Helicopters dropped supplies of rice into the city. People set up guard posts to defend the ministries.

THE KHMER ROUGE ENTER PHNOM PENH

At Depo Market, I met an elderly man named Lok Lien, a doctor, whose daughter had married my brother-in-law. When my brother-in-law went to live with his parents-in-law, I went to live with him. Later on, they fired more and more artillery and one day, my younger brother, a barber, went to live in the vicinity of Santhor Mok. I drove my motorbike to find him. From Santhor Mok to the Central Market, all the cars were turned upside down, and some were under fire. The Khmer Rouge were entering. Because there was so much artillery, my younger brother said he wanted to go back home, to our home village. I told him not to worry about me. If he wanted to, please go! I became terrified living in Tuol Kauk, as 20 or 30 houses were burned down by the artillery. Some people crawled and went hiding in the lake, some were alive, and some were dead. My elder sibling witnessed such incidents, and we moved to Depo Market.

One day at approximately 9 am, Khmer Rouge troops, all dressed in black, entered Phnom Penh. One with a siren drove along Tep Phan Hospital and Depo

Market in a truck filled with weapons they were taking to their base. Some of the soldiers were women and some of them drove trucks. One woman carried a B-40 rocket and threatened a military truck driver who was a Lon Nol soldier. He stopped the truck and ran into the house of a Chinese merchant. Everyone fled. At approximately 1 pm, we went to see their convoy and waved white flags. Everyone said, 'Bravo!' as we waived the white flags. I was cheering, too.

At about 5 pm, the Khmer Rouge made an announcement telling everybody to leave the city. In three days, we could return. They said, if we stayed, we would die because the Americans were planning to bomb the city. There was no need to take any belongings because it would only be three days. The Khmer Rouge soldiers walked along the road and shouted at us to leave, but no one wanted to leave. There were 10 or 15 of them. I decided I had to leave with my family and we took just a small amount of rice with us. Joining us were my older sister, Lok Lien, and Kong Sam-ol, who had married Lok Lien's daughter.

EVACUATION

We headed down the Lok Sang [monk] Hospital road to Dei Hoy [flying dust] Market. I thought that if we headed for Kampot and Kampong Speu, there would be no water. If we went to Roka-kong, there would be water because it was located along the river. So I decided to walk along the river, going Roka-kong. It got dark before we could reach Prek Phneou so we stopped at Kob-srov Dam. We were afraid that if we stopped they would shoot us. It was 7 pm. We went through Tep Phan Hospital and headed through Lok Sang [monk] Hospital Street.

There were masses of people. There were so many people that we could not identify which child was ours and which belonged to somebody else. People got separated. Some children were crying, and some were looking for their fathers. Some were sick and could not speak, and some children helped pull these sick people. It was night time. We could not see each other. We made a tent and Kob-srov Dam.

Other people did the same thing. We cooked rice. We found water by asking around. At dawn, we continued to walk. We walked the whole day, from dawn to dusk. The whole road was packed with people. When it grew dark, we stopped at the Prek Phneou gas station where people were selling fish paste, near the fish farms. It was getting very dark. We cooked, ate and slept on the pavement. In the dark I went out to look for water. The path was narrow and filled with reeds. There were dead bodies all around and I had to walk over them. We could smell the bodies, it was a horrible smell, and it filled the air while we ate and slept. In the morning we saw that we were surrounded by dead bodies, swollen like the carcasses of dogs. We started walking again and we could see the bodies floating in the fish farms alongside the road. The fish were nibbling at them. The bodies in the road had been run over and they were flat like fried bananas, all over the road. Some were wearing military uniforms and others not. Some people just walked over the bodies or drove over them, and others of us carefully stepped around them.

We reached Kruos pagoda and stopped and cooked there. It was around 1 pm. It was really slow going because the road was so crowded. The Khmer Rouge made holes in the road to prevent cars from driving along it and any cars that tried to pass had to go along the bank of the lake. It was very difficult for people to walk or pull carts, and sometimes people had to carry their carts. People said to get rid of any military uniforms because you could be killed if you were military. We whispered this information from one to the other. I had a photo of me from Ratanak Kiri dressed up in a military uniform for fun with rifles and a map. I threw it away. I was carrying a gun and they might have thought I was a soldier, so I threw it into a lake of water hyacinths.

From Kruos pagoda I returned to Kilometer Number Six leaving my wife and children there at the pagoda. I went on alone to find Kong Sam-ol at his house. He wasn't there and so I looked for him along the road because his wife wanted to be reunited with my unit chief's wife, who was her sister. I never found him so I returned to the pagoda. We only stayed in each place for one night. We weren't allowed to stay longer. Some Khmer Rouge searched for people's parents and if they found them they shot them. I don't know why.

We crossed the river by motorboat, but I stayed behind that day because my wife got sick, and one of our children had fever and diarrhea. My brother-in-law wanted to move on, and I said to go ahead and not wait for us because we would meet up soon. His family got into a Khmer Rouge truck and left because the Khmer Rouge were transporting some people. After that there was just me and my family. I had my VESPA but I had just about run out of gas. I had about one liter of gasoline left, but I didn't want to use it.

In the morning I left my children at the ferry and drove my motorbike back to find my wife. There were so many people, walking and driving. My wife got sick. And then my third child, my son, got a fever and died. He was three years old. I borrowed a hoe from people nearby and dug a grave and buried him. But they forced us to keep moving, so we had to leave the next morning.

I dared not leave my children alone during the night. I was afraid of losing them because they kept forcing people to leave wherever they were and move on. In Prek Kdam, after my wife took the medicine, I went and got the children. We ate and spent the night there. By that time, we were almost out of rice. I walked the motorbike alongside my wife and children to Thnal Keong, then through Cheung Chhnok mountain to Skun and turned right toward Cheng Chhnok.

That's where they stopped us. I was taken to Cheung Chhnok pagoda and we spent the night under the house of some elderly people who had been evacuated. Another family lived above us. The next morning, I heard the Khmer Rouge were distributing rice and I went to ask for some. When I got there they asked, "Comrade, how many people?" I told them that we were 5 members, three children and us parents. Then they gave me one can of rice. One can for five people. I began to lose hope when I realized they were giving one can of rice to five people. One can for a whole day. I told my wife I didn't know where we should go. We just had one can of rice left. At night it rained and we slept under the house. There was no cover and the rain fell down under the house, so we went into the kitchen and slept there. In the morning I went to catch crabs in the fields where the frogs were croaking after the rain. Then I went out to find more crabs and met a friend named Saruos. We had known each other at Prey Veng. We went together to hunt crabs at Thnal Keang, where one road led to Skun and another one led to Cheng Chhnok, and we saw a truck filled with sacks of rice, but no one to unload it. I said, 'Comrade, let me unload the rice,' and they said, 'Fine, Comrade, unload the sacks and we'll give you some rice.' After we carried the sacks into the warehouse they said, 'Comrade, do you have anything to carry the rice in?' and I said. 'All I have is my scarf,' and they said, 'Use your scarf and take as much as you want,' and we filled our scarves with rice and put them on our backs and carried them back with us. Each of us almost got one tao of rice, about 15 kilograms. We walked back home happily.

RETURNING TO WORK AS A MECHANIC

The next day, I saw a bus broken down and the Khmer Rouge were using a loudspeaker to say that Angkar needed someone who could fix machines, and could return and work for Angkar. This was at Thnal-bek. I told Ruong that I wanted to go back, and the Khmer Rouge asked me where I had been. I told them I had worked in Phnom Penh and could fix machines. They wrote all this down on paper and gave it to me. But just me. Ruong didn't know how to fix machines. I came again in the evening, and they told me to use the paper and show it those who stopped me and to tell them that Angkar needed me to go back and work in Phnom Penh. Then, suddenly one of them didn't want me to return and I was afraid he might do something to hurt me. At that time, I had a flashlight and I gave it to him along with two shirts and two pairs of trousers. I did this secretly just between the two of us, and he said, 'Comrade you can leave right now or later,' but I had to be out of here by night time.

I went and got my wife and children and we headed back toward Phnom Penh. We joined up with a pilot who had also gotten permission to return and we left together at night. It took us about a week to get back to the city. At the first intersection, it was getting dark and my children were exhausted and we stopped for the night. I told the pilot we would leave in the morning and he said he had decided to stay behind because if they found out that he was a pilot he would be dead. At dawn we headed to Prek Kdam, where I showed the paper to Angkar. There were seven people there who could fix machines. They sent me to work near Kilometer Number Six and I left my family there at Prek Kdam along with the families of the other seven workers.

I returned to Phnom Penh because I knew trucks, tractors, generators, and large and small boat mechanics. At first, Angkar had me go to Office M-11, Water Transport, where I was in small and big boat repair. M-11 was located in Phsar Tauch market and the chief was Morn. I collected and fixed machines for about three months. There were 20 people under the supervision of Sreu, who later was arrested, though I don't know why. Sometimes they arrested someone from a traitorous network, like the Eastern Zone. The group chief was Chham. He didn't know as much as I did, but he was a base person and I was an April 17 person. A base person had the right to kill ten April 17 people. They did not need to ask the big unit or division. When we arrived, there were boats everywhere and soldiers all around. We got to Kilometer Number Six near the milk factory and they put us to work repairing boats in a garage. There were seven or eight usable boats. They were using the boats to transport their troops to Kratie province to prevent the return of the Vietnamese. We worked on those boats for about two months under a chief named Sreu. We didn't have enough food to eat. We had only long loaves of bread instead of rice, we had bananas and we killed and ate dogs. After fixing the boats we were put to work on tractors, a road roller and a truck. They asked if any of us could drive a tractor, and Sreu said, 'Comrade, help drive the tractor onto a boat.' The boat took us to Kratie province, and two or three days later I returned to Phnom Penh. Some people at Kratie knew me from Ratanakiri and wanted me to stay there. But Angkar wouldn't let me stay and told me to go back to Phnom Penh. When I got back I continued to fix boats. There were about 30 of them. They weren't small boats. They could carry tons and tons of milled rice, heading to Stung Treng province.

One day at about 10 am, they came to me and said, we need one comrade to go collect a tractor. They took me at night to O-Russei market and Sreu told me to work there. Out of seven people working there, six died. They killed them all. I don't know where they took them, but they killed them all. I didn't dare say a word. They just disappeared.

WORKING AT O-RUSSEI

After that they sent me to work in the mechanic shop at the State Garment Ministry and they let me take my family to live near me. They divided people into teams, fixing cars and sewing machines. There were 1,000 women making clothes, which were delivered to different cooperatives and provinces. Everybody had to wear black now, and they had to have the black clothes to wear. My wife and my older daughter, who was around 13 years old, were put to work making black pajamas and caps, and I was there to fix the sewing machines. My younger daughter who was about 12 years old lived in the children's unit of Daem Kor Market.

Men and women lived separately. Although my wife and I worked not far away from each other, we were not allowed to communicate. I saw her every day after 4:30 pm when we went to water the vegetables in the ministry's vegetable garden. We did not talk, both of us had our own unit chief, and they were always observing. We looked at each other and gestured to each other quietly. Sometimes we did share one or two words with each other, but if our chiefs caught sight of us they would send us to reeducation.

We both had difficulty because of insufficient food. Sometimes we ate only one course, sometimes we only had one piece of bread. We had to eat separately from each other. She looked weak and thin. Everyone did, not only her. We met once a month, only at nighttime. For that one night, the Khmer Rouge had one room for us, like all couples. I still remember that place where we met once a month. It was a sort of apartment or guest house and they told us what room we could use. It's still there. One night, and tomorrow morning we separate.

In my job at O-Russei they had me fix bicycles, and also lots of other stuff, motorcycles, cassette players and so on. They asked me if I could fix loud speakers and I said I wasn't too good at it, but I could do it. The deputy chiefs there were Kun and Chhum, and they told me to go ahead and work on loudspeakers. They had me walk around the city and collect them wherever I could find them. I had a letter of permission and I could go anywhere and enter any houses. Since I had lived in Phnom Penh a long time I knew which places had loudspeakers. They were at...Phsar Chas, Kandal Market and the Central Market. We took everything because we didn't know which were working and which were not. But all we collected was loudspeakers because that's all we had permission to collect. We got a lot of them, 30 or 40 loudspeakers.

I worked on them at O-Russei Market for about a week and then one day the car of Kun, the chief of Chhum, broke down. The engine would start and then stop. Chhum asked me if I could fix it and I said 'Yes.' When I inspected the car, the driver told me two people had already come to fix the car, but it still didn't work. One mechanic came from Kampong Cham and another came from Kampong Som and still it was broken. I didn't know whether they had let these men go home or sent them to be killed. I saw right away that the problem was with the diesel injection pumps and I took it out and brought it to Chhum. He took it to a spare parts place to the south of the central bus station and brought me back a new one. I cleaned it and oiled it and installed it in the car. I turned on the engine and stepped up a gear for a moment, and it worked. From then on they had me fixing cars instead of loudspeakers.

One day, they had me connect electric wire for broken lamps. I climbed up to connect the wires, but they warned me that I could get an electric shock. I climbed up anyway. I saw that the fuse was not connected and I used two pliers to connect it, and I got a tremendous electric shock. Fire was coming out of my eyes. No one could hear me because of the sound of the generator and I only regained consciousness when I dropped the pliers.

After a month, they told us to stop fixing cars and work in the sewing section. There were just a few workshops at O-Russei and they needed to make thousands and thousands of caps and pajamas. Kun divided people to work in different sections, folding cloth, stitching, and so on. But the people who cut the cloth could not supply it fast enough to the people who sewed it because there were thousands of people sewing. How could they cut enough cloth on time? Kun called me. 'Mey,' he said. He dared not call me 'Comrade,' so he called me by name. He said, 'Mey, what can we do now? We can't make enough clothes quickly enough.' I suggested we use an escalator and I went to find one near O-Russei. There were escalators along the Monivong Boulevard and next to the one cinema. After taking a look, I said I could use the escalator as a model to fold the cloth. I wanted to use the motors, but some were broken and could not be used. So they sent me to a brewery in Kampong Som, the Angkor brewery factory and I brought back some creative ideas. The board of our table was about 1.5 meters and we put them together for about 30 meters. We put the cloth on them and used the motors to pull the cloth. It was like a train. We put the cloth on it and it was cut and then went back and forth. There were piles of cloth and the motors helped us unfold the cloth. After unfolding the cloth we put it on the table, which was about 0.18 meters high and we called in the tailors. The machines were used to draw the legs of trousers. We cut and placed a pattern on the cloth, like the shape of a collar, cloth and drew its outline. Then they took the cloth and we put machines below it to cut it into shape. We could cut up thousands and thousands of meters of cloth in a morning. They put the clothes in a warehouse at the market and people came from around the country to transport them. Can you imagine? Every day people were coming in from every province to collect these clothes. The cloth came from China, just like the oil, gasoline and diesel that we used.

One day I saw the Chinese coming to take photographs of the machinery used to make clothes. Kun showed them around. Another day, Khieu Samphan came in with around his neck and went into the dining hall. He was small, dressed in a black uniform, and had white hair. At that time they had me making cooking pots for a couple of days before I went back to making clothes. Khieu Samphan walked in with two or three people walking behind him. I didn't know who he was, but other people said it was Khieu Samphan, the Khmer Rouge leader. After that I knew who Khieu Samphan was.

We were divided into three groups: candidate, depositee and full-rights people. I was in the depositee group and didn't dare speak up. Depositees were April 17 people who had been evacuated from Phnom Penh and I was the only one in the group. Mostly people who were evacuated from the city never returned. Only technicians returned. We knew we could be taken away and killed any time. People who had joined the struggle were full-rights people, and they could kill us any time. But, we could also build ourselves up and graduate into a higher group. As I remember, three or four people in my group were full-rights people. We were friends with each other and told each other secretly about our status, but it was never mentioned in public meetings. We were careful when we talked. Although we didn't have enough food to eat, just gruel, nobody dared to talk about it.

In late 1977 or early 1978, Kun disappeared. He just didn't come in to work. When he didn't come in for four or five days, we all realized that he had been taken away. I didn't know what had happened to him and I didn't dare ask anybody. After that, more people in the sewing section began disappearing, one after another. Moeun and Dao were taken away. They just disappeared. [An unknown person] was a half Chinese man in charge of writing reports like how much cloth we cut and how many clothes we made. He disappeared. After Kun, Chhum was taken away. Then Yong who came from Laos. He had lived in Ratanakiri when I was there, but he was on the other side. He had been Pol Pot's messenger, and he had taken part in the burning of Bar-keo bridge that I had built. I didn't dare say anything about this. And then he was taken away. And then I was next. We were arrested one after the other.

ARREST

I was arrested on Oct. 28, 1978. My wife and family didn't know what happened to me. And I wondered why they arrested me. I've always wondered about that because I'd never done anything wrong. They tricked me by saying that they needed me to fix trucks near Viet Nam. That morning I arranged my stuff -- my equipment, my tools, my box -- and when I brought it to the car, the Khmer Rouge cadre said, 'Just keep it there. You won't need it.' I didn't expect anything to happen. I was just trying to follow Angkar's orders because you can't deny Angkar. They did not take me to Viet Nam. Instead, they took me to Tuol Sleng [prison].

Three people got into the car, Ta Tim, Ta Try, and me. Lin was the driver. He drove us to a house next to Tuol Sleng. There were Khmer Rouge hiding and ready to arrest us. When we got out of the car, they tied our hands behind our backs and they used my scarf to blindfold me. They walked me somewhere and I asked them to please look after my family. I felt so helpless blindfolded and with my hands tied behind me. I was in the middle of the road and I said, 'Please tell my family I am here,' and they kicked me to the ground and pulled me up by the collar and cursed me and said, 'Angkar will smash all of you.'

They walked me into a room, which is now a reception room at Tuol Sleng. They shackled me, took off my blindfold and handcuffs and began to measure my height. They took a photograph and then they took off my shirt and handcuffed me again. Then they blindfolded me again and took me to a small cell and had me sit on the floor with my legs straight out. They shackled my legs and took off the handcuffs and blindfold, and I sat there on the floor and cried, wondering what I had done wrong.

INTERROGATION

On that same day, at 1 pm, two guards came to my cell. One stood outside, one came in and handcuffed me and blindfolded me again. He pulled me by the ear, forcing me to get up. When they walked me down the stairs they said, 'Stairs. Be careful,' and pulled my ear downwards. They walked me to Building A, and pulled my ear up to let me know there were more steps to climb. They took me into a little room and had me sit on the ground with my legs straight and took off my handcuffs and blindfold. The floor was covered in blood.

It wasn't a big room. There was a desk and on the floor beside the desk was wire, a stick and another stick made out of twisted wire -- you can still see it at the museum. The twisted wire was really strong and it wouldn't break no matter how much you beat with it. They began to beat me, and they kept on beating me for 12 days and 12 nights. Every morning at 7 o'clock I was brought out of my cell to the interrogation room and I was returned to my cell at 11 am. Then from 1 pm to 5 pm, I was interrogated some more, and again at night from 7 pm to 11 pm. Twelve days and 12 nights. Of course it was not like I was beaten the whole time. They beat me, and sometimes they stopped and asked me questions and then beat me again.

They began to question me: 'How many people in your group? Who recruited you to join the CIA?' And I put my hands together and begged them, saying I did not know what the CIA or KGB was. It was true, I had never heard of them. Maybe there really were people who joined the CIA. I don't know about other people they interrogated. At one point I used my hand to block the blows and they broke my little finger. Over again and again, they only asked about KGB and CIA. If I talked about anything else they beat me. 'When did you join the CIA? Who introduced you? How many people in your group?' Over and over. They did not ask if I was a traitor or what I did. They just wanted me to say I was with the CIA and KGB. If I didn't say that, it was the wrong answer.

I was mainly interrogated by Seng and Tit. Seng had light skin, half-Chinese. Tit had dark skin and curly hair. As far as I could tell, they did whatever they could to get the confession. They took any kinds of answer in order to report to their boss. If they didn't, they might disappear themselves. I heard that Seng later died. It might be that he got an incomplete confession and he was killed as punishment. That's why they did all they could just to get answers. So we had to give them the answers they wanted. They would only be satisfied if we confessed. And they didn't like my answers.

Seng and Tit took turns beating me. They beat me until they got tired, and sat down, and then they would start beating me again. And the executioner Hor beat me once. That was right near the end. Hor was the deputy chief of interrogation and he could observe what was going on. I heard him tell the interrogator, 'Brother, he isn't answering you. Give him to me, comrade.' And he folded up his sleeves on both sides, grabbed a stick and beat me 50 times. I held up my hand to block his stick and it broke my little finger. He said, 'You aren't answering. When did you join the CIA and the KGB?' He said that if I didn't answer he would beat me to death.

It was Seng who pulled out my toenail, the big toe on my right foot. It was just Seng and me in the room. At first he had a hard time getting the nail out. He got a pair of pliers and he stepped on my foot and tugged on the nail, but it wouldn't come off. So he twisted it back and forth. It took him a long time and I bit my lip to try to bear the pain. And then he gave a big tug using all his strength and yanked it out. At first, I thought he was just threatening me, but in fact he really did it. I think he wanted to pull out the other big toenail too, but maybe because he saw so much blood on the floor he stopped. After a long time the toe grew back but it was different from the big toe on my left foot.

My feeling at that time was that I knew I would be dead. I was really terrified, and I was scared of being electrocuted. Like I said, I could tolerate the pain from being beaten and having my toenail pulled out, but not being electrocuted. That was too much for me. They attached a wire to my left ear and it was like my head exploded. Kuk-kuk-kuk-kuk-kuk-kuk! My head felt like a machine and my eyes were on fire. I fell on the floor unconscious two times. When I woke up I started telling them what they wanted to hear. At that point, I couldn't tell what was right or wrong. I was so afraid they would electrocute me again, so I made up stories about serving in the CIA, paying homage to their flag, and doing destructive things like pouring acid on the clothes we were making and breaking sewing needles.

And then Seng said, 'You motherfucker! If you had told us all this before we wouldn't have had to beat you.' It was horrible, the electric shock, and that feeling still happens to me when I knock my head, like water flowing through my ear. I become deaf when one part of my ear is closed. Also I had a problem with my left eye. I can see better now because recently the Japanese gave me medicine.

After 10 days of torture, I began to confess. Seng sat at the table and typed. Sometimes he would stop and beat me and then go back and type some more. They had to make me confess because they would be killed if I didn't. So I talked and he typed. I couldn't see what he was writing because I was sitting on the floor. When he was finished, he did not read it back to me, but they made me put my thumb print on it.

During the interrogation they kept me in the small single cell with just enough room to sit down with my legs shackled to the floor in front of me. At that time my back had been beaten so badly that I had to sleep on my side. Afterwards they put me in the big cell with about 30 prisoners in the room. We sat in rows on the ground with our feet shackled to a long iron bar.

We were like animals, not human beings. They gave us ammunition boxes to defecate, and plastic boxes for prisoners to urinate. If any of our waste leaked onto the floor, we had to lick it up. That's how we cleaned the floor for them. If we made a sound by moving our legs, and the chains rattled, they would come and give us 200 lashes. We got ladles of porridge or watery rice soup without rice, once in the morning and once in the evening. It was just enough to keep us alive. When we asked for water they would give us just a little bit, and they would beat us if we asked for more. We were starving. If we could catch a lizard or a rat or even an insect, we would eat it raw. We had to do that in secret because we could be beaten for eating. Sometimes when prisoners were brought back from their interrogation they would lie there moaning, and they would be beaten again for making noise. So no matter how much pain I was in, I remained silent. I started thinking about killing myself, but I had no way to do it.

One night they came and took three people from my row. I was the fourth, and Dy Phon was the fifth. He was a dentist. I knew him. I didn't have any idea what would happen to the people who were taken away. I didn't know anything about the killing. I just knew that a truck came to take prisoners out at night time. Dy Phon whispered to me, 'They are taking them to kill them.' He had been there in the big cell longer than I, but I don't know how long. So we couldn't fall asleep, waiting for the trucks to come. We thought, maybe it's our turn this time. We waited until midnight when the trucks came, and they would pull a prisoner up by his ear to go with them.

FIXING EQUIPMENT

One day after my interrogation was over, Suos Thy came and said, 'Who came here from O-Russei and can fix machines?' and I said, 'Brother, I can do it,' and he said, 'Okay, tomorrow I will bring you new clothes. But don't try to escape!' The next day he brought me trousers and a long sleeved shirt. Probably after the interrogation, Seng told Suos Thy I could fix machines and they needed me to do the work.

So I went to the work shed behind the building and began fixing sewing machines.

Two or three days later Seng, my torturer, brought me a broken typewriter and asked me if I could fix it. I said, 'Wait, brother, let me check,' and I turned the typewriter upside down and saw that one key was not working. The ribbon was broken. I managed to fix it and so they saw that I could do the job. Later on, I fixed two other typewriters. They were old and the keys did not function well, but I got them going again.

To them it was really important to have the typewriters in order to take down the confessions, and so that's why they needed to keep me alive. I don't know if someone else had fixed typewriters before me or what happened to him. I just thought that fixing typewriters was really important to these cadres and I'd better do it. The Khmer Rouge had a saying, 'To keep you is no gain, to destroy you is no loss.' At that time, I think the Khmer Rouge thought that to keep me was a gain for them.

So in the morning, they unshackled me and blindfolded me and handcuffed me and took me out to work. At the workplace, I was shackled by just one foot and not blindfolded. I worked at a wooden table. Sewing machines were piled up one on top of the other and I just took one and fixed it and then took the next one and fixed it. I was so much happier out there working, without a blindfold. In the big cell, I felt like a frog in a well. There were three other prisoners working with me. They were Ung Pech, a mechanic, who was fixing cars at that time. There was Kung, who made chains and shackles, and there was Tuon, but I'm not sure what exactly he was doing. We didn't say a single word to each other. We didn't dare. We were just a few meters from each other, but we didn't talk. We didn't even dare look at each other. The Khmer Rouge were watching all the time. The painters like Vann Nath and Bou Meng were working in a different place and I didn't know them.

I worked not too far from the kitchen and I could smell the cooking smells. They even asked me to help with the firewood. Then they let me keep the crust from the rice they cooked for soup, the hard part. I saved those crusts and shared them with Ung Pech in the shop. I put the crusts in the sewing machine drawer. You can eat them, but you can't let the other brothers see, so I hid them. Twice I had to spit out bits of the crust and hide them when people came to talk to me.

While I was working I could hear prisoners in other cells shouting out and cursing the people who were beating them. 'You fucker! Stop beating me! Just kill me now!' You could hear people begging, 'Please stop. Please stop!' I heard people crying for their mothers. Once I heard a small child crying. That was probably because its mother was taken away to be interrogated.

MOVED FROM SMALL CELL TO BIG CELL

Left: The small single cell of S-21 prison. Photo by kimsroy Sokvisal. 2012

Above: The big cell of S-21 prison. Photo by Kimsroy Sokvisal. 2012

FLEEING FROM TUOL SLENG

I worked there for about two months until the Vietnamese came and liberated the country. We escaped together, the prisoners and the jailers and torturers, maybe 30 people together. I didn't see my interrogators. The situation was in chaos. We did not care who was who. We were all just fleeing for our safety. One cadre came up with a red motorcycle. At that time I was teaching two women cadre how to fix a water pump. There were gunshots and all of a sudden, chaos. They unchained us and took us to the room where Vann Nath painted. They squeezed 18 prisoners into that room. Ung Pech was the only one I knew. Then they brought us out – no blindfold, no shackle, just guards with guns. The man on the motorcycle led us out, and then drove back to kill those last prisoners who were chained to their beds. That's what I learned later from Vann Nath.

They herded us out of S-21 and took us toward Am-Leang district. I had no idea where that was. The guy on the motorcycle told us the situation was not good. They put us in a pagoda and told us to stay there before continuing our journey to Cheung Ek. At that time, we did know it anything about Cheung Ek, even though that is where they would have taken us from Tuol Sleng to kill us. We got there at night and waited while they discussed whether to kill us. But they decided it would take too long. So they led us on to Prey Sar, where other prisoners had been held. All people had left, except a few female cadres.

Then I had a lucky coincidence. My wife was a prisoner there and I saw her holding our two month-old baby. She was there on a watermelon farm, under a sugar palm tree, with about 10 other women. At first I didn't go to her because I was afraid of the guards. I told one of them I would like to go help her carry my small baby, and he said, 'Ok, go ahead and help your wife carry your child.' My wife gave me a scarf and asked me to give it to a woman who was helping deliver a baby under the tree. I dared not speak to my wife because we were prisoners and I was afraid of being beaten. We did not say anything because there were many people around us, and we did not want them to hear us.

Then two Vietnamese trucks and a Land Rover came and began shooting at us, and everyone panicked and ran for safety. I wanted to head back, but someone told me to keep moving. Dy Phon, Bou Meng and Vann Nath escaped when the shooting started, but I was with my wife who had recently given birth to my son so I couldn't run away. I stayed there with her and another prisoner named Eng.

I held the baby and we kept walking down the road and talking, me and Eng and my wife. I asked her why they took her to Prey Sar prison, but she did not know.

She said they took her there to transplant and harvest the rice. I thought it was probably my fault, that I did something wrong and that's why they brought me to Tuol Sleng and arrested my wife, even though she was pregnant. Probably my baby was born at Prey Sar. We were trying to escape and we were tired, so we did not talk much. I did not have chance to tell my wife how I was mistreated and tortured at Tuol Sleng.

When we got to Srah Thol pagoda it was about 5:30 pm and we were hungry. I saw about 50 armed Khmer Rouge cadres and I asked them, 'Comrade, may I have some rice for my family?' They asked about where I came from and I told them I came from a sewing unit in O-Russei and then they asked me about my home, where I came from. I told them I came from the Eastern Zone and after hearing this word, they asked me to wait here until I get a letter from Angkar.

The cadre gave us a place to sleep at the pagoda dining hall. It was me, Eng, my wife and baby sleeping on the bed together. Then the soldiers left secretly. I saw that it was probably about 7 pm because everything became quiet. One soldier was left to guard the place. It was impossible for me to sleep. And so I was awake and I noticed right away at midnight, or 1 am, three cadres arrived armed with AK-47s and one carbine. I heard one of them say, 'Where are those three people we have to kill?' and someone said, 'There they are, sleeping on the bed.'

When I heard the word 'killing', I woke up my wife and Eng. The Khmer Rouge said now we have a letter from Angkar. They told my wife to walk ahead of me and Eng. My wife left first, carrying the baby. Then Eng and then I was the last. We walked slowly, about one kilometer. It was a full-moon night. Suddenly they started shooting. My wife called out, 'Pheap father, run!' (That was what she called me, using the nickname of our oldest child.) Then I heard Eng shout: 'Run Mey! Run Mey! They are killing me.' So I ran for my life and escaped.

When they shot my wife, I could still hear my child crying. I was sure they would kill him, and I knew that if I returned to help my son, they would kill me, too. I kept on thinking of my son, but it would have been useless. After shooting my wife and Eng, they came after me. I hid behind a termite mound and it suddenly became quiet. I thought maybe they had run out of ammunition and were reloading. I crawled away as fast as I could into the paddy field. The soldiers thought I was still hiding behind the termite mound and kept shooting at the hill, but I was already far away. I kept on running the whole night, thinking of my wife and son, and in the morning I hid in the forest.

My idea was to return to Phnom Penh, but I really had no idea which road led to Phnom Penh and which to Am-Leang. On the third night, I met two women who were carrying rice and I asked them 'Comrades, where's Thmat Porng. The women said it was in the opposite direction. I could not move fast because my leg was swollen so it took me another three nights to head back. I walked only at nighttime. For six days and nights I didn't have a single drop of water. It was too dangerous to look for water either at night or in the day time. So I ate thnoeng leaves, which are full of water. You can find those leaves all over Cambodia. Peasants use them to cook sweet and sour soup. So I ate those leaves and kept some in my pocket. When I arrived in Thmat Porng, I saw people drawing an ox cart to their house. It seems that people there were not sleeping in their houses for fear of both Vietnamese and Khmer Rouge troops. So villagers would put their things in the ox cart and slept in the rice fields.

I had to get back to Thmat Porng mountain because that was where I went when I was evacuated from Ang Snuol and then I would know the way back. My clothes were torn because I had been hiding in the forest. When I arrived at Thmat Porng mountain, I saw no one there, although there had been lots of people living there before. I went into one cottage and found a knife. I used it to cut sugar cane and ate it along the way. I was so hungry that I wanted to eat the whole sugar cane, but I could not swallow it because I was starving and it was too much. From there I got a clearer idea of the way back to Phnom Penh. At Kdann Roy, I saw Khmer Rouge soldiers evacuating people to Am-Leang. I walked towards them, knowing I had nowhere else to go, and they asked, 'Comrade, where are you going?' That's when I began to lie. I said I wanted to go to Snaor cooperative. They asked me why and I said I was going there to get my child. But, of course, I had no child there.

When I arrived at Snao cooperative, I lied again and told the Khmer Rouge cadres there I was going to Krel to see my child. It was about 12 km from Phnom Penh. When I arrived in Krel , I met two women, including my future wife, Sam Thoeun. She had worked together with my first wife in the sewing unit at O-Russei. I had not known her at that time, but she knew I had been married to my first wife. She asked if I had seen my wife, and I told her my wife had died.

She asked me where I was going and I told her I was going back to Phnom Penh. The two women asked if they could accompany me to Phnom Penh, and I agreed. Before we set off, we collected a large amount of rice because it was harvest season.

Then we met some former workers of Bek-chan factory, which produced plate. They were heading back to the factory to get their old jobs back. I told them I'd like to join them and work there, too. So we all went. I got a job carrying water and cutting firewood. I made five trips a day carrying water, even though my leg was swollen. The owner of the house where I lived made sugar from palm trees. In the mornings, I drank their sugar palm juice. The palm juice helped reduce the swelling in my leg.

I lived there almost a month, and then Vietnamese troops arrived at the factory and I hid from them in rice sacks. The Khmer Rouge came and shot the Vietnamese truck and set it on fire. I escaped to Prey Daem Speu pagoda, next to Pochentong pagoda. I met Vietnamese troops there, and I could speak a little Vietnamese language, and I told them I was not a member of the Khmer Rouge, but a simple citizen.

At Bek-chan, I told the house's owner my story, how my wife and child were killed, and he arranged for me to marry Sam Thoeun, the woman who had known my wife at work. I had no clothes to change into. Only my torn clothes from Tuol Sleng, so people lent me some clothes for my marriage. This was about one month after I left Tuol Sleng.

My wife is about 20 years younger than I am. The owner said that since I had no family left, and this woman was an orphan with no husband, we both didn't have anyone to rely on. So we had a small ceremony. It was not like a real wedding, just offerings to our ancestors to allow us to live together. But it was a real marriage. Under the Khmer Rouge, they would have 20 or 30 marriages at once, and just exchange a cup of tea. I felt sympathy for her. She had no parents and no way of getting back to her home in Kampong Cham. There were no cars or taxis at that time, only Vietnamese trucks, and no one trusted the Vietnamese. The Vietnamese troops were very hard on women, and I wanted to protect her. We stayed with some other people in their house for about a month and then left for Phnom Penh to find a home and work.

After my marriage, the transportation section of the newly-formed government was looking for people with skills like former mechanics during Lon Nol regime. When I learned about that, I went to work in O-doem, close to Pochentong National Airport and brought my wife to live with me there. There was almost no one in Phnom Penh and I saw only one or two people at first. Then people began to move back gradually. I was assigned to collect equipment and install it in a warehouse.

A TRIP TO GERMANY

In O-doem, in the transportation section, my superiors saw me work very hard, focused and skillful, and they supported me by giving me rice and clothes. I started receiving letters of appreciation from the government. In 1982, the government selected me to go with a group on a trip to East Germany. In Germany, they took us to a Nazi concentration camp. I didn't have any other clothes so I went there only in m green workers uniform. I still have the photograph. We transited through Hanoi and Karachi before arriving in Germany. In Hanoi, there weren't many cars, mostly cyclos. There was only one bridge from Noi Bai airport. In Karachi, the trees had no leaves because it was so hot.

It was winter in Germany. Upon arrival, a woman named Mrs. Kristof pushed me into a car because it was so cold. If we wanted something the sponsors of the trip would buy it for us. They bought us clothes and shoes because we went there without shoes and with no cold-weather clothes. We stayed in a hotel. One thing I saw was how Germans could lift a ship over the mountains and put it into the sea. Then they took us to the highest tower in Berlin. At night they took us to parties where we drank and danced. Of course, I drank and danced as well, but I did not get drunk because we were dancing so much.

The following morning we went to camps where Nazis killed Jews, near the border of Poland. When I was taken to the camp, I thought of Tuol Sleng. There was the same killing in these two places. The difference was at that camp they killed only Jews. It was also different from Tuol Sleng because they had many beds and didn't have to sleep on the floor. They could bathe, too, so Tuol Sleng was worse. We went to Berlin and they let us climb onto a wall to see into other side. They showed me the guard dogs at the wall. They told us how Nazis killed people and showed us a place where people were burned alive.

AFTER RETIREMENT

I lived in O-doem until 1993. When I retired from the Ministry of Transportation, I moved to Sa-la Market, next to Stung Meanchey, and went to work for a businessman named Mong Riththy. I had met him many times and he had asked me to come work for him, so after I retired I asked him for a job. He asked me how much money I wanted and I said $400 a month, but he said that was too much. He was in hurry because he had a plane to catch to Singapore. When he came back I told him I would work for $300.

At that time, my wife did not work and my children were small, but I earned enough to support my family. I have three daughters and three sons in my new family. Two daughters and one son are married. All my children still live with me except for one daughter who lives outside with her husband. Mostly my daughters support me now selling clothes in the market. One son works as a guard and two sons work in Kampong Cham picking mangoes.

Mong Riththy's company was in Phnom Penh, but his warehouse was in Prek Eang, and that is where I worked, traveling back and forth. He said he didn't have any idea about machines, and he put me in charge of all of that, like chief of the warehouse. He kept traveling to Singapore and his business grew. When I started to work for him, he had three tractors and two trucks, but now he's a millionaire and a senator. He bought four or five more tractors, which he used in his project growing palm oil trees. They were huge machines that could uproot big trees. I stayed with him for 12 years, until 2005, and after that I spent another year fixing tractors for other people.

RETURN TO TUOL SLENG

The first time I returned to Tuol Sleng was when an East German film crew gathered seven survivors together for the first time in 1979. During that period only the communists could come to Cambodia. At that time I only knew one other survivor, Ung Pech. The last time I had seen him was at the workshop at Tuol Sleng when he was fixing trucks. I remember that he waved his hand at me and warned me not to talk. So we didn't talk during that time but we shared food. When he got a piece of cake cooked with banana and sticky rice he broke it into two and gave half to me. And when I got rice from rice soup I shared it with him. When the Vietnamese came, Ung Pech was one of our group but we were separated at Ang Snuol when the Vietnamese began shooting at us. That was the last time until we met again with Ung Pech. After liberation they made him head of the Tuol Sleng museum, but later he was sick and went back to America, where he had studied, and died there.

About two years later an American journalist based in Singapore came and interviewed me. We talked from 7 am to 12:30 midday. He gave me five dollars and a box of cigarettes. They were Dunhills. But I'm not a smoker.

In 2002 the filmmaker Rithy Panh was making his documentary about Tuol Sleng, "S-21: the Khmer Rouge Killing Machine." I returned there as well as Vann Nath and Bou Meng, who had been saved because they were painters. There were several people from the Tuol Sleng staff. Prak Khan, an interrogator; Him Huy who was responsible for taking prisoners to Cheung Ek; Suos Thy, who was in charge of paperwork, and Mam Nai, a chief interrogator. Later they all testified at the trial, along with Vann Nath, Bou Meng and me as survivors.

Over the years many journalists and visitors have talked to me at Tuol Sleng, and many people cry when they hear my story and see the tiny cell I was kept in. When I see them cry I cannot stop my own tears from falling. One time a group of more than 15 French visitors came with guides. They could not believe Khmer would kill Khmer and they cried. Duch's defense lawyer Kar Savuth was there and said, "Just tell them what happened to you," and the guide was translating to those French students and then broke into tears and ran into another room. Not only here in Cambodia but around the world people cannot believe that Khmer could kill Khmer.

POSTSCRIPT AT THE KHMER ROUGE TRIBUNAL
Extraordinary Chambers in the Courts of Cambodia (ECCC)

In 2003, nearly three decades after the end of the Khmer Rouge regime, Cambodia and the United Nations established a joint special tribunal to try senior leaders and those "most responsible," like Kaing Guek Eav, known as Duch, on charges of crimes against humanity, war crimes and other charges. Formal proceedings began in 2006 and on Feb. 17, 2009, the first case opened, with Duch, the commander of Tuol Sleng, as the first defendant. Chum Mey attended almost every day, often sitting side by side with Bou Meng, his fellow survivor and fellow civil party seeking at least moral reparation from their jailer.

"If the court can't find justice for me and other victims, then our lives have no meaning," Chum Mey said just before the trial began. "We just die."

That June, just over 30 years after his prison ordeal ended, Chum Mey confronted Duch in court in emotional testimony that mixed tears with anger. "I cry every night," he told the court. "I am like a mentally ill person now."

"The method used was very brutal," he said, describing his 12 days and 12 nights of torture. "There was no hot or cold method, as Duch said. It was always the hot method. And we were called 'despicable this or that.'"

The chief judge, Nil Non, seemed fascinated by the details of the torture.

"And the nail was gone?" he asked, as Chum Mey described his torturer tugging at his toenail with a pair of pliers.

"Yes, the nail was completely detached from my toe," Chum Mey said.

"They twisted the nail with pliers and as it didn't come off, they pulled it out."

"Do you mean the whole nail was pulled or only part of it?" the judge asked.

"The whole nail," Chum Mey said.

"Did the nail grow back?"

"Yes, but it grew deformed."

"Can you show us the deformed nail?" the judge said, and Chum Mey stood and removed his shoes.

"Technician, can you show the feet of the civil party on the screen?"the judge ordered, and the courtroom video zoomed in on the victim's feet.

The judge also probed the technicalities of the electric shocks inflicted on Chum Mey.

"You said these electroshocks were not carried out as described by the accused, that is, with a manual dynamo, but that it was real electric current, 220 volts, that came from the socket – the regular voltage used in offices. Is that correct? And they placed electric wires on your ears?"

Chum Mey said yes.

"The accused stated that electroshocks were carried out only with a hand dynamo," the judge said, pouncing what he saw as a discrepancy. "But in real practice, it seems that interrogators actually used electricity coming from the socket. So, maybe they were acting without the knowledge of the accused."

This was the first time Chum Mey had addressed Duch, whose face he said he had never seen at Tuol Sleng, and his anger flared. "I would like to tell this to Duch," he said, "that Duch did not beat me personally, directly; otherwise he would not see the light of day today."

The judge was quick to jump in.

"Uncle Chum Mey, please be well-behaved and make sure that you be more ethical and try to avoid attacking any individual because it is more about the legal proceedings."

Duch was sentenced in July 2010 to 35 years in prison, a term that was effectively reduced to 19 years when the court took into account his partial cooperation and time he had served illegally in a military jail. Chum Mey was outraged. "I cannot accept this sentence," he cried, addressing clusters of reporters outside the courtroom. "I am not happy at all. We suffered once under the regime and

LEADERS OF DEMOCRATIC KAMPUCHEA (1975-1979)

POL POT
Brother Number One

IENG SARY
Deputy Prime Minister
and Minister of Foreign Affairs

IENG THIRITH
Minister of Social Affairs
and Health Care

NUON CHEA
President of People's Representative Assembly

LEADERS OF DEMOCRATIC KAMPUCHEA (1975-1979)

KHIEU SAMPHAN
President of State Presidium (Head of State)

DUCH
(Original name: Kaing Guek Eav)
Chief of Tuol Sleng prison (Office S-21)

now we are suffering again."

But in February 2012 a higher court extended the sentence to life in prison and Chum Mey said got his first good night of sleep, after years of nightmares.

"As I listened to the verdict being read out I was getting anxious and my heart was thumping," he said. "If the judge had announced that Duch only received 35 years in prison, I would have left that courtroom immediately and withdrawn my civil party application to Case 002 and I would never go to the court again. It wouldn't have been justice."

"I was watching Duch's face as the decision was read out. His face turned black. He was worried. Earlier when he came into the courtroom, Duch always looked for me and Bou Meng, but that day, he only looked down. He probably knew in advance that what would happen. A life sentence.

"When the verdict was read, I wanted to fly off the chair. I wanted to scream but I was afraid the judges would say there's something wrong with that guy. I wanted to scream "Justice is alive. Justice is alive."

Testimony at ECCC

SECTION ON KSAEM KSAN:

In 2010, Chum Mey and a small group of survivors including Bou Meng created a foundation called Ksaem Ksan (the Association of Victims of Democratic Kampuchea) that he said would assure that victims had their own organization once the trial was over and would provide assistance to those in need. "I would use some of the money from this book for members of the association who need help," he said. "If women lose their husbands, or if their house burns down, some amount can be used for help. We will try to foster reconciliation between victims and perpetrators. The vision of our association is neutral, not on the government side or NGO side. We have people who are Khmer Rouge victims. After the court is done, all of its offices will disappear, the victim support section will disappear, but my association will still be in place. We will be transparent to outsiders. Up to now we have 1,600 members and more and more want to join us." From the association's web site www.ksaemksan.info:

VICTIMS ASSOCIATION
OF DEMOCRATIC KAMPUCHEA (KSAEM KSAN)

United in the quest for justice, social harmony, a culture of peace and spiritual healing. March 20, 2010

1- History of the Association

The Association of Victims of Democratic Kampuchea (Ksaem Ksan), or the Ksaem Ksan Association for short, is one of the first Victims Associations in Cambodia. Ksaem Ksan Association was created to give a unified and strong voice to the victims. The idea of creating the Association emerged when the ECCC on August 27 decided without notice that civil parties in Case 001 had no right to question character witnesses in the Duch's trial. At that time, 28 civil parties sent a letter to the judges, signed by all 28 civil parties, protesting that decision and boycotted attendance at the trial's proceedings. On September 13, 2009, 33 civil parties from ECCC Cases No. 001 and 002 gathered at the premises of the NGO ADHOC and decided to create the Ksem Ksan Association. They elected a 9 member standing committee. On January 29, 2010, the Association was registered at the Ministry of Interior. On March 1, 2010, we made a formal request to be registered by the ECCC Victims Support Section. The logo of the Association is a rainbow. In Khmer's beliefs, the rainbow connects the earth to the sky and appears after storms and rains. In Khmer, Ksem Ksan means "peace in mind or serenity". Our Association's vision is serenity in this life and the next life.

2- Members registration and funding

To date, our Ksem Ksan Association has registered 451 members, among which there are 325 women and 126 men, living in 17 provinces. We are attracting more and more members. Each member is asked to contribute the sum of 4000 riels (1 US $) per month but no action will be taken against those members who cannot afford to do so. Our principle is to rely on our own means only for day to day operations. So at each event of the Association, we will ask contribution from our guests, even a small one. For projects which require more financing (we will mention those later), we will organize a partnership of the willing; this is to say, NGOs, government departments, private institutions, individuals etc that are interested in a given project will get together and contribute to its realization.

3- Our guiding principles

As stated in our statutes, Ksem Ksan Association is neutral vis à vis political parties and will not support or subordinate our organization to any institutions, be they political, governmental or nongovernmental. We will welcome any contributions, material and financial, but no links or conditions may be attached other than transparency and accountability in the use of the funds. In this respect, we will establish friendly contacts with other victim's association, in particular with Ms Seng Theary's Association. In addition, membership will be granted regardless of nationality, religious belief, sexual orientation or political affiliation. The only prerequisite for membership is qualification as a victim, as felt by the person concerned. As a member, she or he has to abide by the Association's rules and principles. The Association is a non-profit organization. Members are forbidden to raise money on behalf of the organization, except as directed by the Standing Committee. Under these circumstances, a public announcement will be made on a case-by-case basis.

4- How can we help our members?

Before speaking about how we can help our members, let us define ourselves by the negatives:

We are not a government institutions like the justice system, hospitals or the Red Cross;

We are not a private profit institution like microfinance banking or the utility operators;

We are not an NGO involved in human rights, housing rights, legal rights, or land disputes, or a charity dealing with issues such as health care or domestic violence;

We cannot afford to have too many expenses given the limited means of our members.

So consequently, we will focus on spiritual and/or psychological solidarity. We will help our members recall and document their life events during the Pol Pot regime and share those among members, the ECCC, documentation centers such as DC-Cam and other Victims Associations.

We will discuss and cooperate with willing partners to publish biographies or works from our members such as books or articles with the double purposes of defusing the suffering of the authors and passing on their experience to future generations. We will help devise a pedagogical tool to help disseminate the history of democratic Kampuchea.

In all circumstances, the Ksem Ksan Association will cooperate with both judicial and moral authorities to find ways to alleviate the suffering and to obtain some kind of reparations.

In a broader sense, the Association will convey the message and wishes of its members to the ECCC and other concerned parties, make contact with the donor community in order to improve participation of its members in the ECCC legal process, amplify its cooperation with organizations such as TPO, as well as create a chain of solidarity to help aging and ailing members and organize votive ceremonies according to members' religious belief, whenever possible.

5- Projects and requests

5.1. Preservation of bones at Tuol Sleng and Cheung Ek

We request that the bones already unearthed or to be unearthed at Tuol Sleng and Cheung Ek be preserved and not incinerated. We hope that one day DNA techniques will reveal filiations of these bones with living relatives, enabling family to identify the remains of their loved ones and organize ceremonies in their memory. We reject categorically the idea of incinerating these remains even under religious pretexts.

5.2. Construction of a stele with the names of all 17,000 human beings tortured and assassinated at Tuol Sleng and Cheung Ek.

We support the demand for reparations put forward by the civil party lawyers in all four groups of Case No. 001. One of the demands is the construction of a stele bearing the names of all 17,000 victims at Tuol Sleng and Cheung Ek. In the event that the ECCC does not decide to erect this stele, we will seek partnerships with willing parties to build it and have it inaugurated by the next Pchum Ben.

5.3. Religious ceremony on the date of the announcement of the verdict for Case 001 On the date that the Duch's verdict is announced, we will organize, at Tuol Sleng Museum, a ceremony in the memory of all our victims. The ceremony will probably take place in the early morning of that day, before heading to the ECCC.

Ksaem Ksan Association contacts:
Mr. CHUM Mey (President) Tel: 012 71 21 48 (Khmer Speaking)

Mr. KIM Mengkhy (Lawyer Association)
(Khmer,English,FrenchSpeaking)

Mr. PONN Chamnab (Administration Officer)
(Khmer,English Speaking)
Contact Office: No 61 A, Street 608, Boeung Kak II, Toul Kork,
Phnom Penh, Cambodia
Email: contact@ksaemksan.info
Website: www.ksaemksan.info

Organization Structure:

Mr. Chum Mey (President)

Mr. Chum Sirath (First Deputy President)

Mr. Bou Meng (Second Deputy President)

Mr. Chhat Kim Chhun (Administrative Director)

Mr. Ouch Sun Lay (First Vice Administrative Director)

Mr. Heng Bunnet (Second Vice Administrative Director)

Mrs. Phung Sunthary (Treasurer)

Mrs. Chum Neou (First Vice Treasurer)

Mr. Chhoek Pon (Second Vice Treasurer)

Mr. Seang Vandy (Program Director)

Mrs. Kan Sunthara (Deputy Program Director)

Mr. Kim Mengkhy (Lawyer and Executive Secretary)

Mr. Ponn Chamnab (Administration Officer)

Objective

Participate in all stages of ECCC process in the name of association's member Provide members opportunity to express their joint willing such as to ECCC Spiritual and material support of each other when they meet difficulty situation Improve living level of members.

Outreach to new generation to understand better on the history happened during the democratic Kampuchea regime in order to prevent the rebirth of the regime Combined relevant history of Democratic Kampuchea for sharing to new generation Coordinate for reconciliation in order to improve peace in community claim the justice for victims.

Vision

The Association has a vision of leadership of being the conscience of enhancing the rights of victims. The Association shall endeavor to play leadership role by pursuing with Kampuchea victims reparation programs, social fund, psychological and material support, social harmony, reconciliation, justice, culture of peace.

Mission

Provide legal service such as complaints completion, finding of probono lawyer for victims under the jurisdiction of ECCC Monitor the ECCC's proceeding and verdict enforcement Training, publication and production of film related to Kampuchea Democratic victims Organizing workshop, training and public forum Professional training and organizing for job creation to members in accordance their specialization in order to enhance member's living Endeavor to increase membership upon real case Represent members in accordance law and regulation Victims Association "Ksaem Ksan" set up two accounts as below:

1- Social Fund Account was set up in order to support association's members confronted in emergency such as death, sickness, traffic accident, house burned and/or any other unpredictable circumstances. It is sourced mainly through members donation and generous concerned people.

Account Name : Victims Association of Democratic Kampuchea
(KSAEM KSAN)
Account Number : 00011093100616 (For United State Dollar)
Account Number : 00011093100626 (For Riel)
Bank : ACLEDA Bank Plc., Head Office, Phnom Penh, Cambodia;
SWIFT CODE: ACLBKHPP;
CHIPS UID: 415637

2- Operations Account is separated from the Social Fund account. It is used for the day-to-day operations of the association. The Operation Fund is sourced through national and international donors.

Account Name : Victims Association of Democratic Kampuchea
(KSAEM KSAN)
Account Number: 00011069621018
Bank : ACLEDA Bank Plc., Head Office, Phnom Penh, Cambodia;
SWIFT CODE: ACLBKHPP
CHIPS UID: 415673

Interested generous donors, please send your contribution according to you desire to help either in social funds or in the functioning of the association.

Please take note of both accounts : Social fund account and Operations Accounts as above.

FACT SHEET ON "S-21" TUOL SLENG PRISON

Written by: Dacil Keo; Compiled by: Nean Yin
December 6, 2010

Following the odor of decayed flesh, on January 10, 1979 Vietnamese soldiers drove towards a barbed wired compound that served as the Khmer Rouge regime's highest level security center. At the security center, coded named S-21 ("S" for Santebal, the Khmer word meaning "state security organization" and "21" for the walky-talky number of former prison chief Nath), prisoners were brought in often handcuffed to be photographed, interrogated, tortured, and executed.

The interrogators based their technique on a list of 10 security regulations which included, "While getting lashes or electrification you must not cry at all." Although prisoners often had no idea why they had been arrested, interrogators forced them to confess their crimes. If they did not confess, they would be tortured. However after confessing, they were marked for execution. Initially, prisoners were killed on the grounds of the prison, but as the mass and stench of the corpses rapidly increased and became unbearable, prisoners were then transported en mass to a nearby open field known as Boeung Choeung Ek ("Crow's Feet Pond") to be killed. Often, they were made to dig their own graves or the graves of other prisoners and then killed using rudimentary weapons.

The Tuol Sleng prison, S-21, located in Phnom Penh, Cambodia was a microcosm of the terror, paranoia, and brutality that took place across the country under the reign of the Communist Party of Kampuchea from April 17, 1975 to January 7, 1979. The shocking numbers commonly associated with the prison- 14,000 killed and 7 survivors-rank the prison as one of the most lethal in the 20th century. These numbers however have been disputed by scholars and experts; and recently the hybrid Khmer Rouge Tribunal offered their figures based on its criminal case involving Kaing Geuk Eva, alias Duch, the head of S-21.

The number of prisoners taken to S-21 ranges from the Tribunal's conservative estimate of at least 12,272 to some expert's figure of approximately 20,000. The number of survivors has received less scrutiny however with most of Western media generally accepting the figure of 7 survivors. This figure of 7 has been repeated for over thirty years now, giving S-21 its notoriously brutal image. The origin of this numbers comes from a 1981 film titled, Die Angkar ("The Angkar"), produced by Studio H&S of the former East Germany. In this film, the photograph of 7 survivors of S-21 was shown.

There is some speculation that 7 survivors were shown to parallel the 7th day of January, the "day of victory" in which Vietnamese forces overthrew the Khmer Rouge regime. After several years of research however, DC-Cam estimates that at least 179 prisoners were released from 1975-1978 and approximately 23 survived after VietNam ousted the Khmer Rouge regime on January 7, 1979. The release status of the 179 prisoners (of which 100 were soldiers) is based on numerous Khmer Rouge documents and interviews compiled primarily by Tuol Sleng Genocide Museum senior archivist Mr. Nean Yin. Most of the 179 who were released have disappeared and only a few are known to have survived after 1979. Of the 23 who survived after 1979, more than half have disappeared or have died since. Several of the survivors who are alive today have recently made the news: Norng Chanphal for being a witness for Case 001 of the Khmer Rouge Tribunal, Vann Nath and Chum Mey for being featured in documentary films, and Bou Meng for having a published about him.

The names below (surname first) provides the most up-to-date record of survivors of S-21, both those released before 1979 and those who survived after Viet Nam entered the country. If known, a person's alternate name or nickname is also given in parenthesis.

Child Survivors who were found by Vietnamese soldiers on January 10, 1979.[1]
1. Makara (full name unknown)[2]
2. Name unknown[3]
3. Norng Chanly
4. Norng Chanphal[4]
5. Socheat (full name unknown)

Survivors who are alive today
6. Bou Meng[5]
7. Chum Manh (Chum Mey)[6]
8. Heng Nath (Vann Nath)[7]
9. Nhem Sal[8]
10. Touch Tem[9]

Survivors who died after 1979
11. Eam Chann
12. Phann Than Chann
13. Ruy Nea Kung
14. Ung Pech

Survivors who disappeared (witnesses reported that these men were alive after 1979, but since disappeared)[10]

15. Dy Phon[11]
16. Eng (full name unknown)[12]
17. Leng (full name unknown)[13]
18. Mok Sun Khun
19. Pol Touch
20. Tuon (full name unknown)

Survivors who are thought to be alive, but status uncertain

21. Name unknown[14]
22. Pheach Yoeun
23. Sok Sophat

Prisoners (from Khmer Rouge army division 420) released between 1975-1978 before Viet Nam entered Cambodia[15] (they have since disappeared)

24. Bo Boeun (Phal)
25. Chan Chan
26. Chan Chhoeun (Than)
27. Chea Va (Tva)
28. Chhay Sei
29. Chhim Hin (Sei)
30. Chhoeung Soeung
31. Chhum Bun
32. Chhum Than (Cheat)
33. Chin Seng Eam (Voar)
34. Chum Chan (Khem)
35. Chum Mey (Vorn)[16]
36. Chuob Meng Uor (Chev)
37. Chuon Srei
38. Di Don (Vy)
39. Dib Thau (Rin)
40. Dieb Phan
41. Duong Chheng Pat (Rit)
42. Duong Sambat (Chum)
43. Ean Hun (Hak)
44. Hai Run (Rin)
45. Ham Cheum (Khom)
46. Hang Han (Huon)
47. Hang Lay
48. Hem Muon (Muon)

49. Heng Ruon
50. Heng (Nea)
51. Hing Muon (Vuth)
52. Ho Phan (Phat)
53. Hun Uy (Chhoeun)
54. Huon Samphai (Muon)
55. Huot Sok (Sokha)
56. Im Boeun (Ly)
57. It Aun
58. Keo Lonh Ret
59. Khem Siem Muoy (Peou)
60. Khuon Tai Eng (Lan)
61. Khut Krauch
62. Kim Leng (Heng)
63. Lach Saom
64. Lach Sarun (Van)
65. Lim Uong (Vin)
66. Lom Lon
67. Mak Thoeun (Thon)
68. Mam Vin (Bol)
69. Meas Lan (Loeun)
70. Meas Noeun (Theng)
71. Meas Set
72. Meun Chin
73. Miech Phon (Phal)
74. Neou Nan (Ol)
75. Nhem Chhon
76. Noem Nem (Sim)
77. Nok Nan (Nem)
78. Nou Chhoeun (Sit)
79. Nouv Samneang (Van)
80. Oeur Phat (Roeun)
81. Pak Thiev (Thon)
82. Pan Kung
83. Pat Fy (Yang)
84. Pech Soam
85. Pen Tak (Van)
86. Phal Nhoeun (Khan)
87. Phauk Sam (Sim)
88. Phon Sun (Srun)
89. Poan Pin

90. Prak Samnang (Tep)

91. Prik Chhon (Rung)

92. Prum An (Rai)

93. Prum Leap (Yan)

94. Sam Mak (Rin)

95. Sam Rith (Hang)

96. San Mab (Ma)

97. Seng Hun (Hat)

98. Seng Yan (Oeun)

99. Siek En (Kren)

100. Soam Phon (Nan)

101. Soeng Tha (Vorn)

102. Srei Yun (Sdaeng)

103. Suon Oeun (Der)

104. Suos Ram (Pheap)

105. Suy At

106. Suy Kim Sat (San)

107. Suy Than (Sim)

108. Svay Kenh (La)

109. Te Na (Thy)

110. Tep Sary (Ran)

111. Thab Ruon

112. Thi Than

113. Thlang Rin (Rum)

114. Uk Van

115. Um Voar (Yi)

116. Un Sao (Sen)

117. Van Ngauv (Pan)

118. Ven Chamroeun (Yen)

119. Yan Yeun

120. Yang Khe (Seang)

121. Yem Yoeun

122. You Han (Phal)

123. Yu Mon

Prisoners released from 1975-1978 before Viet Nam entered Cambodia[17] (only a few are known to have survived while the vast majority has disappeared)

124. Beng Pum

125. Bou Ngorn Ly

126. Cheng Srorn

127. Chhean Vik

128. Chheang Pech
129. Chheang Praing
130. Chhem Chan
131. Chhiev Sun Heng
132. Chhim Pauch
133. Chou Pin
134. Dai Peng
135. Ea Chhai Pauv
136. Ea Ho[18]
137. Ea Kok
138. Han Nhauv
139. Hem Sambath
140. Hin Chi
141. Hong Chin
142. Ik Chheng Eang
143. Im Phal
144. Im Saom
145. Khiev Eng
146. Khlauk Sran
147. Khon Kuoy
148. Kim Sruo
149. Kong Van Tha
150. Kong Van Than
151. Kruy Cheat
152. Kry Sok Heng
153. Lao Seng Kim
154. Long Neng
155. Men Ol
156. Meun Yeng
157. Mi Sri
158. Min Kan
159. Muo Pech
160. Muong Ny
161. Muy Ruos
162. Ngin Hon
163. Nhem Man
164. Noeu Pheap
165. Pa Chhun Try
166. Pao Chheng
167. Pech Muom
168. Pech Phuong

169. Phai Yim
170. Phan Yoeun
171. Pheng Oeun
172. Pong Pan
173. Prach Torn
174. Proeung Si Ieang
175. Ring An
176. Roeun Leng
177. Sa Ke
178. Sa Sam Ang
179. Sam Sas
180. San Khmao
181. San Song
182. Sao Voeun
183. Saom Song Heang
184. Saut Chhorn
185. Seang Kry
186. Seth Kalkhann[19]
187. Sim Yeng
188. Sin In Ny
189. Sla Dek
190. Ta Chi Veng
191. Tao Kim Huy
192. Thong Nget
193. Tim Kim Eang
194. Tim Sy
195. Ting Hai
196. Tit Chuon
197. Tit Kan
198. Try Chak
199. Try Chea
200. Van Yeng
201. Ven Sovan Ny
202. Yun Loeun

[1] The discovery of these five child survivors was captured on video footage by Ho Chi Min City Television (HTV). Two of the five child survivors, brothers Norng Chanphal and Norng Chanly, publically confirmed their S-21 imprisonment status.

[2] Makara was named by a Vietnamese soldier after the Khmer word for January, when Viet Nam entered Cambodia.

[3] This prisoner, a baby, died upon discovery by Vietnamese soldiers on January 10, 1979.

[4] Norng Chanphal was a witness for Case 001 of the Khmer Rouge tribunal involving head of S-21, Duch.

[5] Bou Meng is the topic of Huy Vannak's book titled, "Bou Meng: A Survivor from Khmer Rouge Prison S-21, Justice for the Future, Not Just for the Victims," published by Documentation Center of Cambodia, 2010.

[6] Chum Mey was featured in DC-Cam's documentary film, "Behind the Walls of S-21: Oral Stories from Tuol Sleng Prison" (2007) and Rithy Pan's documentary film, "S-21: The Khmer Rouge Killing Machine."

[7] Vann Nath was featured in Rithy Pan's documentary film, "S-21: The Khmer Rouge Killing Machine." **He died on September 5, 2011.**

[8] Person claims S-21 prisoner status, but there are no supporting documents.

[9] Person claims S-21 prisoner status, but there are no supporting documents.

[10] Interview with Heng Nath aka Vann Nath.

[11] Dy Phon's confession at S-21, cited in Irene Sokha's article in Searching for the Truth (Jan. 2000).

[12] It is possible that this is the same person as #60 (Khuon Tai Eng) or #145 (Khiev Eng) on the list.

[13] It is possible that this is the same person as #62 (Kim Leng) and #176 (Roeun Leng) on the list.

[14] DC-Cam was informed of a former S-21 prisoner currently living in Ratanak Kiri province but there are no supporting documents.

[15] The status of these prisoners has been confirmed through DC-Cam's archives.

[16] Not to be confused with Chum Mey #7 on the list).

[17] The status of these prisoners has been confirmed through DC-Cam's archives.

[18] Ea Ho filed a civil party complaint to the Khmer Rouge tribunal through DC-Cam.

[19] Seth Kalkhann, who has an Arab father and Lao mother, was sent to S-21 with his family and an Indian family on April 11, 1976. The published report, "People's Revolutionary Tribunal Held in Phnom Penh for the Trial of Genocide Crime of The Pol-Pot-Ieng Sary Clique (August 1979)" (Foreign Languages Publishing House, 1990), gives an arrest date for Seth (April 11, 1976) but not an execution date. DC-Cam's senior researcher Dany Long discovered and interviewed him on August 27, 2008. In the interview, Seth states that he was imprisoned for a month, made to write an autobiography, and beaten. His family was kept in a separate room. After a four-hour meeting with Khmer Rouge cadres, Seth and his family were sent back to Prek Dach commune, where they had been evacuated to on July, 1975.

LISTS OF BOOKS, FILMS AND DRAMA

A SELECTION OF BACKGROUND ABOUT CAMBODIA AND THE KHMER ROUGE

This book is the latest in dozens of memoirs by survivors of the Khmer Rouge years, many of them written by refugees who were children between 1975 and 1979. It is the third by a survivor of Tuol Sleng prison, following books by Vann Nath and Bou Meng.

Here is a selection of memoirs and biographies, followed by a selection of books on the Khmer Rouge as well as Cambodian history and culture. A brief list of documentary films includes (three) that include Chum Mey: Behind the walls of S-21, Inside Pol Pot's Secret Prison and S-21 The Khmer Rouge Killing Machine.

MEMOIRS AND BIOGRAPHIES:

Becker, Elizabeth. Bophana, Phnom Penh: Cambodia Daily Press, 2010.

Bizot, Francois. The Gate, London: Vintage, 2004.

Chandler, David. Brother Number One: A Political Biography of Pol Pot, Boulder, CO: Westview Press, Inc.,1992.

Fifield, Adam. A Blessing over Ashes: The Remarkable Odyssey of My Unlikely Brother, New York: HarperCollins, 2000.

Him, Chanrithy. When Broken Glass Floats: Growing Up under the Khmer Rouge, New York: W.W. Norton and Co., 2001.

Himm, Sokreaksa S. with Greenough, Jan. The Tears of My Soul: The Story of a Boy Who Survived the Cambodian Killing Fields, London: Monarch, 2003.

Himm, Sokreaksa S. After the Heavy Rain: The Khmer Rouge Killed His Family. He Tracked Them Down – But Not for Revenge, London: Monach, 2007.

Lim, Bun T. Surviving Cambodia, The Khmer Rouge Regime, Bloomington, IN:Trafford Publishing, 2007.

May, Someth and Fenton, James. Cambodian Witness: The Autobiography of Someth May, New York: Random House, 1986.

McCormick, Patricia. Never Fall Down, New York: Balzer + Bray, 2012. (Story of Arn Chorn Pond).

Nath, Vann. A Cambodian Prison Portrait, One Year in the Khmer Rouge's S-21, Bangkok: White Lotus Co.,1998.

Ngor, Haing. Survivor of the Killing Fields, London: Chatto and Windus,1988.

Ngor, Haing and Warner, Roger. Haing Ngor: A Cambodian Odyssey, New York: Macmillan, 1988.

Schanberg, Sydney H.. The Death and Life of Dith Pran, New York: Viking Penguin, 1985.

Short, Phillip. Pol Pot: Anatomy of a Nightmare, New York: Henry Holt and Co., 2004.

Ou, Chhalith and Halleson, R.Z.. Spare Them? No Profit. Remove Them? No Loss. : The True Story of a Young Teenager in Pol Pot's Cambodia, Lincoln, NE: iUniverse, 2010.

Pa, Chileng and Mortland, Carol A.. Escaping the Khmer Rouge: A Cambodian Memoir, Jefferson, NC: McFarland & Co., 2008.

Pok, Rattana. When Slaves Became Masters, Bloomington, IN: AuthorHouse, 2008.

Pran, Dith. Children of Cambodia's Killing Fields: Memoirs by Survivors, New Haven: Yale University Press, 1997.

Picq, Laurence. Beyond the Horizon: Five Years With the Khmer Rouge, New York: St. Martin's Press, 1989.

Samphan, Khieu. Cambodia's Recent History and the Reasons Behind the Decisions I Made, Cambodia: Ponleau Khmer, 2004.

Seng, Vatey. The Price We Paid: A Life Experience in the Khmer Rouge Regime, Cambodia, Lincoln, NE: iUniverse, 2005.

Siv, Sichan. Golden Bones: An Extraordinary Journey from Hell in Cambodia to a New Life in America, New York: HarperCollins Publishers, 2008.

Soeun, Saroeurn. Scars of a Lifetime, Mustang, OK: Tate Publishing, 2007.

Ung, Bunhaeng and Fox, Martin Stuart. The Murderous Revolution, Bangkok: Tamarind Books, 1986.

Ung, Kilong. Golden Leaf, A Khmer Rouge Genocide Survivor, Portland, OR: KU Publishing, LLC, 2009.

Ung, Loung. First They Killed My Father: A Daughter of Cambodia's Remembers, New York: HarperCollins, 2000.

Ung, Loung. Lucky Child: A Daughter Reunites with a Sister She Left Behind, New York: HarperCollins, 2005.

Ung, Loung. Lulu in The Sky: A Daughter of Cambodia Finds Love, Healing, and Doubble Happiness, New York: HarperCollins, 2012.

Vannak, Huy. Bou Meng: A Survivor from Khmer Rouge Prison S-21, Phnom Penh: Documentation Center of Cambodia, 2010.

Vitandham, Oni. On the Wings of a White Horse: A Cambodian Princess's Story of Surviving the Khmer Rouge Genocide. Mustang, OK: Tate Publishing, 2005.

Yathay, Pin. Stay Alive, My Son, New York: Touchstone, 1987.

Yimsut, Ronnie. Facing the Khmer Rouge: A Cambodian Journey. (Genocide, Political Violence, Human Rights), New Brunswick, NJ: Rutgers University Press, 2011.

HISTORY AND ANALYSIS:

Beang, Pivoine and Cougill, Wynne. Vanished: Stories from Cambodia's New People under Democratic Kampuchea, Phnom Penh: Documentation Center of Cambodia, 2007.

Becker, Elizabeth. When the War Was Over: The Voices of Cambodia's Revolution and Its People, New York: Simon and Schuster, 1986.

Bekaert, Jacques. Kampuchean Diary, 1983-1986, ??: DD Books, 1987.

Brinkley, Joel. Cambodia's Curse: the modern history of a troubled land. New York: Public Affairs, 2011.

Chanda, Nayan. Brother Enemy: The War After the War, San Diego: Harcourt, Brace, Jovanovich, 1986.

Chandler, David. A History of Cambodia, Boulder, CO: Westview Press, 2007.

Chandler, David. The Tragedy of Cambodian History: Politics, War, and Revolution since 1945, New Haven, CT: Yale University Press (1993).

Chandler, David. Voices from S-21: Terror and History in Pol Pot's Secret Prison, Berkeley: University of California Press: 1999.

Ciorciari, John, D. The Khmer Rouge Tribunal, Phnom Penh: Documentation Center of Cambodia, 2006.

Dunlop, Nic. The Lost Executioner, the Story of the Khmer Rouge, New York: Walker and Co., 2006

Dy, Khamboly. A History of Democratic Kampuchea (1975-1979). Phnom Penh: Documentation Center of Cambodia, 2007.

Ea, Meng-Try. The Chain of Terror: The Khmer Rouge Southwest Zone Security System, Phnom Penh: Documentation Center of Cambodia, 2004.

Ebihara, May M.; Mortland, Carol A.; and Ledgerwood, Judy. Cambodian Culture since 1975: Homeland and Exile, Ithaca, NY: Cornell University Press, 1994.

Etcheson, Craig. After the Killing Fields: Lessons from the Cambodian Genocide, Westport, CT: Praeger Publishers, 2005.

Etcheson, Craig. The Rise and Demise of Democratic Kampuchea, London: Pinter Publishers, 1984.

Heder, Stephen and Tittemore, Brian. Seven Candidates for Prosecution:

Accountability for the Crimes of the Khmer Rouge, Phnom Penh: Documentation Center of Cambodia, 2004.

Hinton, Alexander Laban. Why Did They Kill?: Cambodia in the Shadow of Genocide, Berkeley and Los Angeles: University of California Press, 2005.

Kamm, Henry. Cambodia: Report from a Stricken Land, NY: Arcade Publishing, 1998.

Keyes, Charles F.; Kendall, Laurel; and Hardacre, Helen. Asian Visions of Authority: Religion and the Modern States of East and Southeast Asia, Honolulu: University of Hawaii Press, 1994.

Kiernan, Ben. The Pol Pot Regime: Race, Power, and Genocide in Cambodia under the Khmer Rouge, 1975-79, New York: Vail-Ballou Press, 1996.

Kiernan, Ben. How Pol Pot Came to Power: Colonialism, Nationalism, and Communism in Cambodia, 1930-1975, Second Edition, New Haven, CT: Yale University Press, 2004.

Maguire, Peter. Facing Death in Cambodia, New York: Columbia University Press, 2005.

Meng-Try Ea and Sorya Sim. Victims and Perpetrators? Testimony of Young Khmer Rouge Comrades, Phnom Penh: Documentation Center of Cambodia, 2001.

Ponchaud, Francois. Cambodia: Year Zero, New York: Henry Holt & Co., 1978.

Shawcross, William. Sideshow – Kissinger, Nixon and The Destruction of Cambodia, New York: Pocketbooks, 1979.

Van Schaack, Beth; Reicherter, Daryn and Chhang, Youk. Cambodia's Hidden Scars: Trauma Psychology in the Wake of the Khmer Rouge, Phnom Penh: Documentation Center of Cambodia, 2011.

Vickery, Michael. Cambodia: 1975-1982, Boston: South End Press, 1984.

Widyono, Benny. Dancing in Shadows: Sihanouk, the Khmer Rouge, and the United Nations in Cambodia, Lanham: Rowman & Littlefield, 2008.

PHOTO BOOKS:

Cougill, Wynne with Pang, Pivoine; Ra, Chhayran; and Sim, Sopheak. Stilled Lives: Photographs of the Cambodian Genocide, Phnom Penh: Documentation Center of Cambodia, 2004.

Cougill, Wynne with Pang, Pivoine. Vanished: Stories from Cambodia's New People under Democratic Kampuchea, Phnom Penh: Documentation Center of Cambodia, 2006.

Lambray, Maureen. War Remnants of the Khmer Rouge, New York, Umbrage, 2011.

Neveu, Roland. Cambodia the Years of Turmoil, Bangkok: Asia Horizons Books, 2009.

Neveu, Roland. The Fall of Phnom Penh, 17 April 1975, Bangkok: Asia Horizons Books, 2009.

FILMS:

Behind the walls of S-21: Oral Stories from Tuol Sleng Prison by Documentation Center of Cambodia (2007).

Bophana: A Cambodian Tragedy directed by Rithy Panh (1996).

Cambodia Dreams directed by Stanley Harper (2009).

Duch, Master of the Forges of Hell directed by Rithy Panh (2012).

Enemies of the People directed by Thet Sambath and Rob Lemkin (2010).

Facing Genocide: Khieu Samphan and Pol Pot directed by David Aronowitsch and Staffan Lindberg (2010).

Inside Pol Pot's Secret Prison (The History Channel, 2002).
Khmer Rouges Amers (Bitter Khmer Rouge) directed by Bruno Carette and Sien Meta (2007).

LAND/WATER/RAIN directed by Mam Kalyanee with Documentation Center of Cambodia (2012).

Mass Graves Near Pagoda directed by Leng Ratanak with Documentation Center of Cambodia (2011).

S-21 The Khmer Rouge Killing Machine directed by Rithy Panh (2003).

The Khmer Rouge Rice Fields: The Story of Rape Survivor Tang Kim directed by Youk Chhang with Phat Rachana, Documentation Center of Cambodia, 2004.

DRAMA:

Breaking the Silence directed by Annemarie Prins with AMRITA PERFORMING ARTS and Documentation Center of Cambodia (2009).

 (KHMER) SPELLINGS

ខ្មែរ	English
ភូមិគ្នោតច្រោះ	Thnaot Chroh village
ល្វា	Lvea
ស្រុកកំពង់ត្របែក	Kampong Trabek district
ព្រៃវែង	Prey Veng
ស្រុកបាភ្នំ	Ba Phnom district
ស្វាយឧត្ដម	Svay Udom
កែក	Ka-ek
អ៊ិត	It
យក្ស	Yak
នួន	Nuon
ម៉ុំ	Mom
ម៉ន	Morn
ប៉ីអរ	Pei Or
បាភ្នំ	Ba Phnom
ឈើកាច់	Chheu Kach
បឹងស្នោរ	Boeng Snaor
ព្រំខ្សាច់	Prum Khsach
ដើមគ្នោត	Daem Thnaot
ស៊ុំ	Sum
ភ្ជុំបិណ្ឌ	Pchum Ben
បន្សុកូល	Baing-skol
បុណ្យផ្កា	Bon-phka

ឧណ្ណាឡោម	Unalaom
តារារិទ្ធិ	Dararith
ព្រះអន្លុង	Preah Anlong
រកាកោន	Roka-kong
ហ៊ីម	Him
ព្រែកតាអ៊ិត	Prek Ta-it
ទឹកថ្នល់	Tik Thnal
រៀន	Roeun
ដើមក្រខុប	Kra-khop tree
ផ្សារតូច	Phsar Tauch
បុស្សីកែវ	Russei Keo
អូរបុស្សី	O-Russei
លុន	Lung
គុយ	Kuoy
កុឡា	Kola
តាកូន	Takuon
លំផាត់	Lumphat
អូរយ៉ាដា	O Ya-da
អុន ញ៉ាច	Ong Nhach
បរកែវ	Bar-keo
មណ្ឌលគិរី	Mondulkiri
ស្ទឹងត្រែង	Stung Treng
ខ្លុង (ដើមឈើ)	Khlong (tree)
ព្រែកតូច	Prek Tauch
ជីប ឆេងប៊ុន	Chip Chheng Bun

កំពង់ឆ្នាំង	Kampong Chhnang
សំ សារ័ន	Sam Savorn
ជុំ សុភាព	Chum Sopheap
ជុំ កាណាឌី	Chum Kanady
ជុំ ផល្លា	Chum Phalla
ស្វាយរៀង	Svay Rieng
បាត់ដំបង	Battambang
កំពង់ចាម	Kampong Cham
សាលាសន្ធរម៉ុក	Santhor Mok school
ថ្មដា	Thma Da
ច័ន្ទ រស្មី	Chan Reangsey
កំពង់សិលា	Kampong Seila
ម៉ី លី សេង	Mey Ly Seng
កប់ស្រូវ	Kab-srov
តេព ផន	Tep Phan
ដេប៉ូ	Depo
ឡុក លៀន	Lok Lien
ទួល គោក	Tuol Kauk
គន់ សំអុល	Kung Sam-ol
ព្រែកញ្ញៅ	Prek Phneou
ថ្នល់ កែង	Thnal Keong
ជើងឆ្នុក	Chheung Chhnok
ស្រុ	Sreu
ដើមគរ	Daem Kor market
កុន	Kun

ខៀវ សំផន	Khieu Samphan
សួស ធី	Suos Thy
ប្រាក់ ខន	Prak Khan
សេង	Seng
ទិត	Tit
ឌី ផុន	Dy Phon
ជើងឯក	Chheung Ek
ព្រៃសរ	Prey Sar
ថ្មតពាន	Thmat Porng
ធ្នើង	Thnoeng
អមលាវ៉ន	Am Leang
ក្ដាំងរោយ	Kdaing Roy
បែកចាន	Bek-chan
អូរដើម	O-doem
ម៉ុង ឫទ្ធី	Mong Riththy
មៀន	Moeun
ដៅ	Dao
វត្តស្រះថុល	Srah Thol pagoda
ថ្មតពាន	Thmat Porng
អន្ធស្នួល	Ang Snuol
សហករណ៍ស្នោ	Snaor cooperative
សហករណ៍ក្រែល	Krel cooperative
ព្រៃដើមស្ពី	Prey Daem Speu
ព្រែកឯង	Prek Eng
បានលុន	Banlung

រួង	Ruong
ហ៊	Hor
ស្វាយ ក្រវាន់	Svay Kravann
ក្តាន់រយ	Kdann Roy
ព្រៃដើមស្ពឺ	Prey Daem Speu
ផ្សារ សាឡា	Phsar Sa-la
អន្តស្នួល	Ang Snuol
អ៊ុង ប៉េច	Ung Pech

▛▜ CHUM MEY'S CONFESSION

(with introduction by David Chandler and Youk Chhang)

Chum Mey's detailed "confession," like nearly all of the ones from S-21 that I have read, is a mixture of verifiable data (such as the details of his pre-1975 career, minus the "treason") and what must be seen as forced inventions, such as the "crimes" he committed as a garment worker and his supposedly incriminating list of sixty-nine acquaintances as members of his counter-revolutionary forces.

Chum Mey composed this text in response to intense interrogation and continuous torture between 28 October and 9 November 1978. It is one of 5,019 confession texts from S-21, now on microfilm, at the Documentation Center of Cambodia (DC-Cam).

The format of the confession follows the format of most confessions at S-21 that I have read. It begins with Chum Mey's pre-revolutionary autobiography and goes on to relate his anti-Communist treasonous activities (which he says began in the 1950s!). It ends, as most confessions do, with a list of alleged accomplices—in this case, running to sixty-nine names, including those of people he has not seen for many years.

The text, deftly translated by Rich Arant from Khmer, is an excellent example of this terrifying literary genre. It is also the first "confession" published in full in English, and fits nicely with the recently published book by Huy Vannak and Seth Mydans called Bou Meng.

This confession, I believe, will give readers a clear view not only of the life and character of this resilient, courageous, and intelligent Khmer, but also of the cruel and macabre operations of S-21. Without the slightest corroboration, which will almost certainly never become available, Chum Mey's alleged activities as a CIA agent can be rejected out of hand. At the same time, the abject tone of these pages, which can be traced to the prolonged torture that Chum Mey endured, will give readers an idea of the extreme physical and psychological pressures that prisoners, like Chum Mey at S-21 and thousands of others elsewhere in Cambodia, were forced to endure between April 1975 and January 1979.

Above: My life was spared when Seng, my interrogator, had a prisoner carry this typewriter to me and asked me whether I could fix it. I said, "Brother! Wait, let me have a look." After I fixed it, Seng put me to work as mechanic and gave me food. This typewriter kept me alive until the Vietnamese and liberation troops came. Because of this typewriter, I have been able to tell millions of people of the bitter and most brutal operation of Tuol Sleng prison. Photo by Kimsroy Sokvisal, 2012.

THE CONFESSION

D19061 (TSL), C.184
Translated by Rich Arant
Chum Manh, alias Mey
Company Member at the State Garment Ministry
Arrested 28-10-78, 47 years old
Chum Manh
28-10-78
Responses of Chum Manh, alias Mey
Position: Company Member at the State Garment Ministry
Regarding
Personal History of Activities Betraying the Party
9-11-78
Done on 8 -11-78
I request to report to the Party about my personal history of traitorous activities.

My original name is Chum Manh. My alias is Chum Mey. I am 47 years old, and married. Before my arrest, my position was Member of a Company [Committee] on the Youth [Yuvoan] side at the State Garment Ministry. I was born in Boeng Snao Village, Lovea Subdistrict, Kampong Trabèk District, Prey Veng Province, East Zone. My father's name was Chum. He is deceased. My mother's name was Tèt. She is deceased. There were eight children in the family: two sisters and six brothers, two of whom are deceased.

When I was six years old, my mother died, leaving me behind. When I was ten years old, I went to live with my oldest brother named Èk at Phnom Khsach Sâr before my father died. When my father died, I lived with my brother Èk, making a living working the rice fields, farming, and cutting firewood for sale to the Chinese living nearby. When I was 16 years old, my brother Èk died. When I was 18 years old, my Aunt Pol, whose husband Mâpp worked the rice fields, took me to study Buddhist teachings and be ordained at Watt Svay Udâm for one year. After one year, I left my robes and went to study driving in Phnom Penh without letting my siblings and aunt know, because I had left my robes without anything to depend upon since none of my siblings or my aunt had enough to eat. When I first arrived in Phnom Penh, I did not know anyone at all. I had 60 riels at the time, and I walked around the markets to find work as a hired driver. Then I saw a vehicle with only a driver named Tĭt with no driver's helper. I asked Brother Tĭt to let me work with him. When I worked that truck with Brother Tĭt, the thăokè [business owner] who owned the truck was Thăokè Tek, whose house was north of the Independence Monument. Tĭt had me study auto mechanics. I worked the truck and studied at the same time for several years. My salary was entirely up to Brother Tĭt, but Brother Tĭt supplied me with everything, including clothing and food, and he gave me three to four hundred Riel, enough for pocket money up until 1960 when I received 1,000 Riels a month from Thăokè Tek. Then I went to work on trucks in Kratie and in Phnom Penh because Thăokè Tek helped move timber from Steung Treng to Phnom Penh. Brother Tĭt and I began to love one another like brothers, and when we drank coffee in the markets, Tĭt often told me, "Today our country is partially communist already, and the communist regime was very difficult, like it is in China today. The Chinese eat canned food and have no rights or freedoms at all. They have no rights: going out to play, watching movies and plays, dancing and singing, or playing around with girls, they could do none of that. When they go anywhere, they have to ask permission first. If permitted, they can go; if refused, they cannot. It is not like it is with us in a free regime, where we can go anywhere and can make a living as we please, play as we please, buy what we please, do anything as long as we have the money." Tĭt's educating me began in approximately 61 or 62. After Tĭt educated me, he asked me, "Mey, what regime do you like?" I said if it was like that, I liked the free regime and did not like a communist regime because everything was difficult and there were no rights and freedoms. So, Brother Tĭt said, "Mey, if you like the regime of the free world, work with me and help go around making propaganda with those we know well so they will hate the communists and keep them from joining the communist side, work at what they call defending the free world regime. And Mey, if you do this work with me, our boss will give us a raise in salary too." After that, I worked for Brother Tĭt going around making contact with the cyclo workers and trade workers whom we knew and making propaganda about this with one after another. I kept bringing up the communist regime in China, saying that it was difficult to eat and to move around and there was no freedom in making a living. I spoke and stirred up propaganda in the mornings when we drank coffee together. At that time, I did not yet know what to do. I just knew to oppose the communists. I did not yet know about Thăokè Tek. After I made propaganda, I reported to Brother Tĭt. I went around contacting workers, making propaganda all along so they would hate communists; this began during 1962 or 63. Each time I met with Thăokè Tek, he told me, "Strive to work with Tĭt, and I'll give you another raise in salary." He gave me 500 Riels every New Year.

In about 64, after the demonstration attacking the American Embassy, Brother Tĭt called me to the house of Thăokè Tek. Then Brother Tĭt reported to Thăokè Tek that he had contacted me and I had volunteered to serve the free world. Then Thăokè Tek set up a table with flowers on the table and placed a many-starred flag in front of us, and he announced my entry into the CIA. Thăokè Tek told me that the flag, the American flag, represented the free world, and he had me state my resolution to serve the CIA for life. After I made my resolution, Thăokè Tek had me make contacts and conduct activities with Brother T t and Brother Hĕng, a "corporal supervising workers for Tek," to make propaganda to the workers and the people that we knew so they would dislike the communists and like the free world and help make contacts and gather up forces to join the CIA. After joining the CIA, I contacted Brother Tĭt and Brother Hĕng to carry out activities as instructed by Thăokè Tek. In the period before 70, Brother Hĕng still supervised workers cutting timber and trucking workers at Steung Treng. Brother Tĭt still drove trucks transporting timber from Steung Treng to Kratie. As for me, I was a truck mechanic at Kratie, but if trucks were out of repair, I came to Phnom Penh too. While in Phnom Penh, I carried out propaganda activities and made contacts to build six forces after I had joined the CIA and up until 70. There was Hoeun, an ice seller at the Tuol Kouk Market, and Chân, Huon, Thoeun, Vĭn, and Phy, all five of whom were cyclo workers. I have no grasp of them at present. I built all six of them together with Brother Tĭt, and I built them by myself as well, because during the wet season timber could not be transported and the trucks were brought back to Phnom Penh to carry soil until the dry season, when they returned to transport timber. When each person had been built, Brother Tĭt reported to Thăokè Tek, and each of those that had been built met with Thăokè Tek, and then he inducted them into the CIA. As for Brother Hēng, he went to supervise workers cutting timber, and he built forces among the timber cutters. As for the forces that Brother Hēng built in 1970, I have forgotten all their names because I only learned of them each time Thăokè Tek called meetings to report activities and I never made direct contact with any of those forces. I carried out continuous activities making propaganda so the workers would hate communists and continued building CIA forces under the leadership of Thăokè Tek, but by 67,68, 69, Tek instructed me to make propaganda opposing the Khmer Rouge, telling me how Khmer Rouge served the communists and served the Viet Cong, how the Khmer Rouge opposed Prince Sihanouk and were vicious and arrested people and cut their throats with palm stems, how they arrested people and hit them with hoes, how they had no rice to eat and ate only manioc and leaves, how they had no homes to live in and lived in the mountains and in the forests. During 67, 68, and 69, Brother T t and I led the forces we had built, Phy, Hoeun, Thoeun, Chân, V n, and Huon, in carrying out activities in Phnom Penh making propaganda among the workers and those we knew, so they would hate the Khmer Rouge, bringing up what Thăokè Tek had instructed. As for Brother Hēng, he was active among the timber-cutting workers, making propaganda and building forces, and if he saw any Khmer Rouge, he reported them to the forestry bosses in Kratie who came up to measure the forests that had been cut, so the forestry bosses could contact the military in Kratie to go up and capture them. But as far as I knew, they never captured anyone.

In 70 at the time of the coup, the timber cutting stopped. Tek came to make a living by transporting dirt in Phnom Penh. Brother Hēng and Brother Tĭt came to live and drive trucks for Tek in Phnom Penh. As for me, I worked as a truck mechanic for Tek, still north of the Independence Monument, but my house was at Boeng Prêk, near the television antenna tower. By about mid 70, Tek called me, Hēng, Brother Tĭt, Yun, and Choeun—these last two were truck assistants whom Brother Hēng had built—to a meeting and party at his house. Before the eating and drinking, Tek brought up a plan to carry out activities later on in 70: 1) Try to make contacts and build [train up] many CIA forces to help carry out activities to oppose the Khmer Rouge. 2) Make propaganda among cyclo workers, truck coolies, and other workers and those we knew, to make them hate the Khmer Rouge and oppose the Khmer Rouge and to make propaganda to keep them from running off to liberated territory. Beginning in 70, 71, 71, when I went to drink coffee in the mornings, I made propaganda with friends and acquaintances, saying that the Khmer Rouge and the Viet Cong could not fight us and win, telling them to just look at how the North Vietnamese have fought the Americans for so very long and they still have not beaten the Americans. When the Viet Cong attack Cambodia, they are without tanks, aircraft, large and small weapons. How can they win militarily if the Americans help finish it? Also, I made propaganda that when the Viet Cong see our people coming out of the cities, they capture them and cut their throats with palm frond stems, kill us with hoes, cut open our stomachs and stuff them with grass, killing everyone, leaving no one alive. Through this propaganda, most of the cyclo workers and my acquaintances dared not return to their home districts for fear the revolution would kill them. My force-building activities from 70 until 73 created a number of forces: Chèm, Vân, Oeun, Chhēng, and Mân, all cyclo workers whom I built while I was eating and drinking with them. Ouen was a taxi driver at the Phsar Thmei. I have no grasp of any of them at present, because we have been apart since 75. As for Brother Hēng and Brother Tĭt, they were active in driving trucks like I was, and in 72, Brother Tĭt and Brother Hēng took me to meet and make contact with two of the forces they had built, Phēng and Huon, taxi drivers at Phsar Thmei, to have them establish contact and join in propaganda activities opposing the Khmer Rouge and the revolution. I reported all these activities to Brother Hēng and reported to Tek every month.

In about 73, Thăokè Tek called me, Brother Tĭt, Brother Hēng, Chèm, and Phēng to a meeting at his house. Tek gave instructions that in the current situation, many of the people and the workers were leaving Phnom Penh for the countryside, so we all had to make propaganda so they would not continue to leave the cities. We had to make propaganda that those who had left the city for the countryside had all been killed by the Viet Cong, that all who had left the city had been killed to the last man, that the countryside controlled by the Viet Cong had no rice or anything to eat and they ate the leaves from the trees, that the rice fields could not be worked either, because aircraft came and bombed every day, and that if some fields were worked, the Viet Cong took it all anyway. Also, we had to strive to build many additional CIA forces. Beginning in 73, Brother Tĭt and I made contact with one another to lead the forces which had been built —Mân, Phy, Chân, Vĭn, Hoeun, Thoeun, Phēng, Oeun, Chhēng, Vân, Chèm and Huon—to make propaganda so more of the people and the workers would not leave the city, and we brought up what Tek had instructed, to make propaganda among acquaintances through friends who were workers and petty traders in the markets. These activities were continuous until liberation in 75. As for Brother Hēng, I was not very active with him, because he left at dawn with the trucks. As for me, I reserved my free time to work the trucks with Brother Tĭt. So then, for all the activities there was just Brother Tĭt reporting to Brother Hēng or Brother Tĭt and Brother Hēng reporting directly to Thăokè Tek. As for the owner Thăokè Tek, I did not know much about where his contacts were made, because during the day he was not at home much; he went out and disappeared. I only saw a first lieutenant, a soldier who went back and forth to his house, and according to what Brother Tĭt told me, this soldier lived at the Banteay Sloek near the Phsar Daem Kôr. I am not clear about his name. Our important activities before 75 were making propaganda saying that the revolution would not defeat the Americans.

At liberation, we all separated from one another and were evacuated to who knows where. As for me, I was evacuated along the road to Prêk Kdam. When I reached Prêk Kdam, I saw Thăokè Tek for a moment when he was pushing a vehicle being evacuated along the Prêk Kdam road, but we were far apart and Tek did not see me. When I was evacuated to Prêk Kdam, one of Angkar's trucks appealed for workers to return to Phnom Penh, and I returned, because I knew trucks, tractors, generators, and large and small boat mechanics. At first, Angkar had me go to Office 11, Water Transport, where I was in small boat repair.

At Office 11 at that time, there were more than 20 of us. Sreu was in charge. Now he has been arrested. My team chairman was Chhăm, and he has also been arrested. After liberation all my old contacts were broken off. In the high water months of 75—I don't recall the month—Comrade Chhăm took me to find some coffee at Brother Sreu's place south of the Au Russei fuel depot. While drinking coffee, Brother Sreu asked me, "Look, we used to live in Phnom Penh. Which regime was easier, the old regime or the current regime?" I said the current regime was easier than the old regime. Brother Sreu said, "The old regime was easier, how is the new regime easier when we can't even find food to eat? Mey, don't you see that now we eat one piece of bread per meal? Who get to eat their fill? The work is day and night without rest. Who has the strength to work, and there are no salaries, no women, no alcohol, no movies or plays to watch anymore either. In the old regime, we had rank and salary, women and alcohol, movies and plays to watch, rights to move about freely as we pleased, no need to talk about just a coffee to drink. Mey, how do you see it?" I had not yet replied, because I was afraid of him and did not know what his intention was in talking like this. I just responded, "It's up to Brother—whichever side Brother says is easier, I will take that side as well." Brother Sreu said, "Now, Mey, you strive to work a little more, and I will have you promoted to section chairman, squad chairman, with rights to move around and watch them work. You have to do as I say, whatever I say to do." He said to work without paying any mind, just to get it off our hands, to let the revolution grow poor, and when there were many of us, we would rise up and demand to bring back the old regime. And if something came up, to contact Comrade Chhăm and he would know of it, but not to talk recklessly, to maintain tight secrecy. When I returned, I worked following the instructions of Brother Sreu when I repaired small and large boats. I threw away welding rods, sometimes half-lengths. I used gasoline wastefully, using two or three liters to wash my hands each time, and threw away all over the place the metal bolts, cutting up and ruining many of them. At the time, I thought that if Brother Sreu clearly trusted me he would let me be section and team leader with the others, but I did not yet know how Brother Sreu was, and I did not yet know Comrade Chhăm either. Later on, Brother Sreu once again called me and Comrade Chhăm to his place. Then he said, "I feel very sorry for you, Mey. I want to promote you to section and team leader, but I cannot yet do so because we are 17 April people. But in a little while you will certainly be promoted. I have seen that you, Mey, have worked well, as I have instructed. Now, strive to keep on working with Comrade Chhăm and Comrade Phat. The squad chairmen have been arrested and have disappeared already. We must do whatever it takes to damage the revolution, to destroy in every way we can, such as destroying gasoline, destroying bolts and welding rods, grease, electric fuses, and we must slow down and not be too fast. Also, help to agitate and gather up many forces to our side, especially anyone who was liberal before and not very satisfied with the work. If you can make contact, Mey, you must let Comrade Chhăm or Comrade Phat reeducate them, since, Mey, you are a 17 April person and they don't have much faith in you and will not listen well. If we have Comrade Chhăm and Comrade Phat reeducate them, then they will come along quickly." Finally, he said, "Mey, strive to work until we win, and we will certainly become senior people and be comfortable." After Brother Sreu reeducated me, I furtively asked Comrade Chhăm, "What do they call our group?" Comrade Chhăm said, "We are CIA forces embedded inside the revolution to destroy the revolution." I said, "So, is there anyone leading our forces from above?" Comrade Chhăm said, "The leader above us is Brother Sreu, and above Brother Sreu there is Brother Mân, who is in charge of the Water Transport Ministry Committee." From that time on, I knew my group were CIA forces embedded inside the revolution, and I joined in activities with Comrade Chhăm and Comrade Phat in repairing large and small boats and repairing, spilling and wasting, and throwing away both old and new bolts, throwing away keys, using half the grease then throwing the rest away, bending new metal bolts, making engines short-lived and quick to fail by not tightening screws, leaving them loose, and doing repairs slowly, cutting the metal used to patch the boats so large pieces remained, and by throwing away welding rods. As for gathering forces, I personally made contact with older workers Èk, Sâm, and Suon, the most liberal, to complain about not getting to eat our fill, and I reported this so Comrade Chhăm could reeducate and build them into forces to oppose the revolution. After Comrade Chhăm reeducated them, Èk, Sâm, and Suon participated in activities with me in cutting metal to make boats leaving large pieces and throwing them all away, not storing them well. Also we joined in welding and throwing away half-length welding rods.

After repairing small motorboats in Krauch Chhmar district in upper Kampong Cham—I can't remember the month—the water was going down then, Brother Sreu called me, Comrade Chhăm, and Comrade Phat to his house once again. At first, Brother Sreu asked me what I had done in the past period of time. Comrade Chhăm reported that he had attracted three forces, Sâ, Èk, and Suon. Other than that, Comrade Chhăm reported on the activities destroying supplies and delaying the work like I have reported above. Then Brother Sreu instructed us to strive further, especially to attract and build forces. At the same time, we were to strive to destroy every section to the utmost, especially engines and supplies, to do whatever it took to not allow the Water Transport Ministry to operate in the future, and in doing this we were to know how to really consider things and be vigilant to break secrecy. About ten days after receiving the plan from Brother Sreu, at about nine at night, Brother Sreu called me to his house to tell me that State Materials had proposed that I [Mey] go to help tell them about the truck and tractor supplies for a little while, for just one night. I went to Kun's place at Au Russei. After one week, Brother Kun told me, "Comrade, you need not go back. I have already made a request to Comrade Mân and Comrade Sreu, and they are letting you stay right here." Brother Kun had me go work on the vehicles of the State Garment Ministry. I worked on the vehicles from then on.

In early 76—I don't remember the month—I went to get my wife at Office 11, and met Brother Sreu. Brother Sreu asked me how it was, being with Brother Kin. I said it was OK, that he had me work on the vehicles at the State Garment Ministry. He said, "That's good. Strive to work, and if any thing comes up, contact Brother Kun, since I have already told Brother Kin about you, Mey, about you having joined in activities with me. It's OK. Brother Kun is one of us too. Mey, strive to work. I am here working at Water Transport." When I returned to State Garments, I did not immediately meet with Brother Kun. About one month after that, Brother Kun had one of our comrades at Office Kôr 9 (C-9) call me to meet him at Office Kôr 9 during the night. Brother Kun asked me, "How goes it? Have you taken your wife to meet Comrade Sreu?" I said that they had met. Then a jeep arrived at Office Kôr 9, and Brother Kun had me go to my work place first, and wait to see him again on a later day. Two days passed, and I went to Brother Kin's place. At the time, Brother Kun asked me, "When you went to get your wife, did Brother Kun say anything?" I said, "Brother Kun told me that if anything came up to contact you, Brother: he said that you were like him." He said, "Now, Mey, you must continue these activities, and if there are problems, make contact with Comrade Săo, Comrade Saut, Comrade Phăn, Comrade Răn, and Comrade Chhum. Everyone in this group is with us, cooperating in activities. But, Mey, in particular you must keep constant contact with Comrade Săo, because he is in charge of the vehicle section, but you must also maintain secrecy. Be vigilant against breaking secrecy, or else all of us will die."

1. Brother Săo: From the North. Back then he was the chairman of vehicles at State Garments. Now Brother Kun has moved him to the State Warehouse: I have no grasp on what job he has there.

2. Comrade Saut: Chairman of the lathe shop, State Garments. Already arrested.

3. Comrade Phăn: Chairman of construction at State Garments. Already arrested.

4. Comrade Răn: Chairman of Cambodian medicines, State Garments. Already arrested.

5. Brother Chhum: Chairman of Office Kôr 9, State Garments. Already arrested and disappeared.

After meeting with Brother Kun, I made contact with Brother Săo. He instructed that we had to carry out activities on vehicles, destroying oil, gasoline, diesel, engine oil, to doing whatever it took to ruin them. Second, we had to destroy grease, keys, mallets, pliers, chisels, hammers, saw-sharpening files, drills, to smash them to bits and not let the revolution have them for use later on. Third, we had to delay work and stir up the masses about not getting to eat their fill and working without rest. Fourth, we had to stir up the masses and persuade them to attract many more forces to us at the State Garments Ministry. And we also had to act with Comrade Hoeun (past unknown, from the North, now at the sewing machine warehouse) and Comrade Hat (team chairman in carpentry and vehicles, now arrested). Later on, Comrade Hat and I made contact with one another and acted to stir up the masses saying that Angkar was very strict, that we had strived to beat the enemy and now we worked day and night with not enough food, so who had the energy to work? After being agitated, our comrades went around complaining about not getting to eat until we were full. Aside from these activities, Comrade Hat and I destroyed oil, like bringing in much engine oil and not using it all, and leaving it to be rained on. Gasoline and diesel was used wastefully to wash hands and was not kept for further use; it was used for washing and then thrown away. Usable bolts were taken off and thrown away; fasteners and nails, saws were broken; keys were thrown into the sand. Lightly-used files and grease were thrown away. Bolts were turned until the threads were stripped, or they were left untightened. Hat and I carried out these activities constantly, both destroying and delaying the work, with Brother Săo leading. Another activity with Hat and me was impeding transport, causing the trucks to break down constantly, breaking down every three days, setting the carburetors so the fuel would not ignite. Aside from this, Hat and I made contact with Comrade Hoeun to conduct activities at the lathe site. After I had damaged vehicle parts, they were taken to Comrade Hoeun to lathe and he did not follow the forms, making them smaller or larger until they had to be filed down or made into something else, using up a lot of time and burning up two lathes by leaving the electricity on or not using enough electricity, and breaking lathe bits, breaking saws, and breaking drill bits one after another. At this same time, in 76—I can't remember the month—Comrade Hoeun took me to contact two of his forces: 1) Try, then a combatant in lathes and before his arrest a deputy team leader; 2) Comrade Thân, from the North, at that time chairman of a lathe team, and now a combatant in lathes at the State Garment Ministry. Contacting these two was in order to carry out activities breaking lathe bits and drills bits by placing pressure on the bits while turning, causing them to dig deeply and break. In late 76, Brother Sǎo told me of one of Brother Kun's forces named Lon. Comrade Lon was then in charge of a spearhead gathering up state materials. Before arrest, he was Youth Chairman at the State Garment Ministry. But at that time, I had not yet make direct with Comrade Lon. Comrade Ran, Comrade Phǎn, and Chhum were the same as Comrade Lon: I had not yet made contact with them, because I made contact up above at the level of Brother Sǎo, and Brother Sǎo had direct contact with Comrade Kun and Comrade Lon, Comrade Ran, Comrade Chhum.

Around late 76, Brother Kun moved Brother Sǎo to the State Warehouse for good. After Brother Sǎo went to the State Warehouse, Brother Kun appointed Comrade Thol in lathes to come to the vehicle section. Then Comrade Hoeun told me that Comrade Thol was a force of Brother Saut too and to make contact with him. "Thol has been arrested and has disappeared." Several months later - I had not yet contacted Comrade Thol - when Comrade Thol called me and Comrade Hat to meet him. He said, "Our past activities have been constant, so we have to continue these activities further and strongly. We have to especially concentrate on our work in vehicles, destroying in every way, from small things up, so that Angkar will find things difficult to solve. At the same time, we have to stir up the people not to concentrate on work, to be complicated about not eating their fill, eating food that was not tasty, working too much, not playing and moving around freely, so that we could build forces in the vehicle section to come to our side. But now Angkar is setting the direction to transport soil to plant vegetables and support the ministry, so we have to find a way to impede this with the trucks, not letting the trucks go to carry soil, so that Angkar's plans will not be a success." Later on, Angkar went on the offensive moving soil to plant vegetables. Comrade Hat, Comrade Thol, and I strove to carry out activities on after another, mostly by turning the bolts to let air into the carburetors so the vehicles would not start, so the trucks could not carry much soil since they were broken down and would not start, causing the wheel bearings to break for lack of grease, breaking the axles, burning up the clutches, causing the engine breakers to burn up. In early 77, Comrade Hat and I attracted two forces, Comrade Hiem and Comrade Srâs, drivers:

1. Comrade Hiem: I have no grasp of his past. Now he is a deputy driving team chairman at the State Garment Ministry.

2. Comrade Srâs: A driver combatant at the State Garment Ministry; he has already been arrested.

Both of them were bored with their work, and at that time they had to get up to transport soil starting at 2 or 3 am and they became complicated, so Comrade Hat reeducated them. I did not reeducate them much because the masses did not listen to me much. Comrade Hiem and Comrade Srâs conducted activities after being reeducated, and they damaged trucks frequently by not filling oil and by destroying batteries by not filling battery acid, burning up clutches, and burning up fuses and dynamos. Comrade Hat and I were attached to Thol for only about two months when Thol had to go back to lathes, and Brother Kun assigned Hēng to come from the production site to be in charge of vehicles. Hēng has now been arrested. Next Angkar arrested Brother Kun, and the female Khân, the former ministry deputy chairwoman, was promoted to be ministry chairwoman. Khân has already been arrested and has disappeared. Comrade Hat and I had known Brother Hēng from when Brother Săo was there. He had told us that Brother Hēng was a force of Brother Kun too, but I had not yet been able to make contact. When Brother Hēng came to be in charge of vehicles, Comrade Hat and I made contact, and then Comrade Hoeun further told Comrade Hat and me that Brother Hēng was one of the forces on our side and to go ahead and make contact and not be afraid. A while after Brother Hēng came, he called Comrade Hat and me go to a meeting at night in front of the garage. Then Brother Hēng asked Hat if Comrade Hoeun had told him anything. Hat said the Houen told me to contact Brother Hēng, who was a force on our side. Brother Hēng said, "In the past, Angkar has arrested a number of our forces, like Brother Kun for instance, but even after the arrest of Brother Kun our forces still remain. Look at Sister Khân, our Ministry Secretary: she is one of our forces too. As for the forces lower down, we have made contacts and gathered up many of them. We should not yet lose hope. We still have forces in lathes, in folding and cutting, in medicine, and in electroplating. We still have forces in buttons, and we have many forces in the fishery too." When he finished talking, I asked who are forces were in each section. Brother Hēng said there were more than a few, such as Ta Y, Comrade

Ngoeun, Comrade Chean, Comrade Nhăm, Comrade Chhăm, Comrade Chhun, Comrade Loeum, Comrade Long, and Comrade Noeun.

1. Ta Y: Former tailor, but don't know where he went. He came from North Zone Garment. Now folding and cutting chairman.

2. Comrade Ngoeun: Past unknown. From the North. Now the boxing and cutting team chairman at State Garments.

3. Comrade Chean: Past unknown. From the North. Now a combatant in carpentry at State Garments.

4. Comrade Nhăm: Past unknown. From the North. Now a team member in carpentry at State Garments.

5. Comrade Chhun : Past unknown. From the North. Then in State Garment fisheries. Now a platoon member at State Garments.

6. Comrade Chhăm: Past unknown. From the North. Then in fisheries along with Chhun. Now a platoon chairman at State Garments.

7. Comrade Loeum: Past unknown. Now team chairman in buttons.

8. Comrade Long: Past unknown. In the Office along with Brother Kin and Brother Chhun. Now a team chairman in electro-plating at state Garments.

9. Comrade Noeun: Past unknown. From the North. Now a deputy platoon leader at State Garments.

Brother Hēng continued, saying, "We must continue activities in our spearheads. The other spearheads are following their tasking. We in the vehicles spearhead must carry out vehicular activities. We destroy in every fashion possible, from small screws on up, doing whatever to impede work in the ministry so that it cannot prosper. And we strive to make contacts and build many additional forces in each section so that our forces will outnumber those of the revolution. Furthermore, we must stir up the masses to become more complicated, to keep work from progressing and to facilitate attracting forces as well."

After receiving plans from Brother Hēng, Comrade Hat and I, Comrade Hiem, and Comrade Srâs constantly carried out activities in vehicles, from oil, screws, bolts, saw-sharpening files, chisels, destroying by being wasteful and by discarding.

Breaking saws when sawing, discarding chisels not the least worn out, using lots of grease, and discarding it before it had been used, and taking off slightly worn engines and discarding them, and damaging batteries, circuit breakers, dynamos, bearings, oil filters, which were items not easily found. Comrade Hiem and Comrade Srâs did not fill up with oil or water or battery acid for urgent work and caused the vehicles break down frequently. Brother Hēng destroyed 300 sets of trousers and shirts in the warehouse by giving acid to Phăt, the wife of Comrade Lot at the warehouse to sneakily pour on the clothing.

In approximately mid-77, Lon called Hēng to a meeting in a house in front of Office Kôr 9, with Sister Khân and the female Von, in charge of the women's section at State garments, now arrested and disappeared. After the meeting was finished, Brother Hēng called me, Comrade Hat, Comrade Hoeun, Comrade Long, Comrade Loeum to a meeting in a house in front of the Au Russei garage, a vacant house. Then Brother Hēng asked for each section to report what activities had been done. Hoeun reported that he had burned up two lathes and had damaged some screws, had broken about ten lathe bits, had and had also broken drill bits, saws, and files, and had worked slowly, not following Angkar's plans. Comrade Long said that his electroplating team had damaged sewing machine bobbins, sewing machine bobbin keepers, and had burned up a number of sewing machine drive wheels, chrome was not brought since the fluids were not correctly mixed, destroyed water buffalo hide for burnishing. Loeum reported that his side was active damaging plastic grinding machines by putting keys to break the machines and spilling and wasting plastics, breaking one button press. Comrade Thân reported that he had damaged one case of bolts by letting them get rained one and rusted, and had also destroyed an additional number of saw blades, chisels, files, lathe knives, drill bits. In vehicles, Comrade Hat reported destructive activities, including pouring out and discarding oil, throwing keys, saws, files, chisels, bolts, and discarding some vehicular equipment, causing vehicles to break down frequently by driving them without adding oil and without adding enough water. It was reported that each section had not yet built forces, and Brother Hēng said, "In the past some of us have been arrested by Angkar, but now we have consolidated completely in buttons, in vehicles, in lathes, in electroplating, in folding and cutting, in fisheries, and we have carried out activities in each section – like in folding and cutting with Comrade Ngoeun and Ta Y, and in fisheries with Comrade Chhăm, Comrade Chhun, where they have been active constantly too, with Comrade Lon in the lead. Therefore, in the future, following the instructions of Comrade Lon, and Sister Khân, all of us will continue to carry out activities including destructive activities in each section, delaying activities, counter-revolutionary incitement activities, and building our forces. And we must concentrate the most on building forces and on destruction, especially in lathes an in electro-plating. If we can totally impede those sections, we can impede the ministry, because the important thing in our ministry is garments. In Garments, if we can impede the machines, what could go forward? But we have to vigilant of the enemy in all these activities, feeling things out and looking both to the front and to the rear." When the meeting ended, everyone went back to their sections to carry out activities.

After receiving these plans, Hat and I destroyed four vehicle batteries by not adding enough acid, causing them to burn up after use, burned up the bearings in two large trucks, broke two axles because of not having greased them, broke four spark plugs, discarded oil filters, discarded kralâ prang, and increasing the electricity to blow out headlights, causing continuous damage, acting once every ten days after having damaged the engines which had been collected in the spearheads and not reporting to Angkar, not replacing, not letting the masses know. Another activity was Hat and I contacting Hoeun, Noeun, Long, Try, Ngoeun, Loeum, Hiem, to agitate our comrades in the masses in the sections by saying that Angkar had not solved their livelihoods enough, letting them eat fish past and fish sauce, and bragging that how could a socialist regime be comfortable if there was not enough food and we could not move around even a little bit. Also some of our comrades went to watch movies, and some went to greet visitors. We incited them by saying, "Look at Angkar. Some comrades get go to watch movies, some go to greet visitors, and some all not allowed. How is that equality, if some comrades go and some are not allowed to go?" We all worked together and stirred up the comrades who did not go to watch movies or greet visitors, saying that Angkar did not trust them, if Angkar trusted them they would have gone, but Angkar only trusted the only group chairmen, the team chairmen, who got to go. We in the masses did not yet to go with them. After being stirred up, a number of the masses pretended to be sick and did not go to work since they did not get to see the movies or greet visitors. Some slept one day and did not work. Others were complicated and worked just to get it off their hands.

In about mid 77, Yong came to take charge of the State Garment Ministry. Now he has been arrested. At that time, Khân had already been arrested and the Ministry Committee had been reorganized with Brother Yong, Comrade Von, and Comrade R n from the Southwest.

When Brother Yong came to take over as ministry secretary, I was worried and afraid that secrecy would be broken and it would reach me too, because Khân had already been arrested by Angkar, and I assumed that Brother Yong was a revolutionary. But in July or August 77, I asked Brother Hēng and Hat, "How it will go for us, when Angkar has arrested Khân and someone new had come to be ministry secretary? What did we think about this?" Brother Hēng said, "Don't worry, Khân is really gone, but Brother Yong is still here. Brother Yong is not a force of the revolution, but is on our side. His arrival to lead the ministry makes it easy. Keep on striving to carry out activities. But do whatever to appear to be legitimate: don't let them notice us conducting activities. After that, I don't remember the month, Brother Hēng called me, Hat, Ta Y, Ngoeun, Thân, Hoeun, Long, and Noeun to a meeting in a vacant house in front of the Phsar Au Russei garage, and Brother Lon attended as well. Lon and Brother Hēng had us report on the activities done by each section. Initially Long reported that his electroplating team had damaged a large number of sewing machine tension take-ups, bobbins, bobbin-keepers, and drive wheels, the electro-plating team not making them bright, leaving them to burn up, and damaging the plating solution. Then Noeun reported on the activities with buttons along with Loeum, damaging the button grinders and breaking one button press. Thân reported that his side had damaged 200 welding rods and some bolts by letting them get rained on, and they had damaged files, saws, drill bits, sharpening stones, and lathe bits. Hoeun reported on the activities done like Thân's and building two forces, combatants, Comrade Pech and Comrade Thea. Comrade Pech is now a team chairman in lathes at State Garments. Comrade Thea now is a combatant in lathes at State Garments. Both of them formerly came from the North. Later Comrade Ngoeun reported activities in folding, cutting, and sewing. He worked with Ta Y to cut garments leaving large pieces of scrap, burning up one pair of electric scissors, sewing clothing and breaking many needles and working slowly, not as quickly as Angkar had directed. Finally, Hat reported on the activities done in vehicles with me and Comrade Hiem that I reported above. After the reports were finished, Comrade Lon said that our activities had been carried out at every spearhead, so we had to continue according to our capabilities. We would do as much as we could, large or small, but we had to be vigilant to not allow any further break in secrecy. If anyone was arrested, they would have to be responsible for themselves and not implicate anyone at all. In the immediate future, we would build additional forces to grasp the totality of each section. If the ministry is ours, the sections are ours; we can do whatever we wanted, because they are all our people. After the meeting - I don't remember the month - Brother Yong moved me to study working on sewing machines. After I went to study working on the sewing machines, Brother Hēng came to see me, and he instructed me, "Today Angkar is having the ministry go on an offensive to make garments for distribution to the people in the Zones and to repair machines for supplying the Zones. Now, Brother, you must attract Ta Vet, the sewing machine repairman. If you can attract him it will be easy for us to block a large part of the work of the ministry, because the sewing machines would be ours, the repairmen's. If we let them sew, they can sew; if not, they cannot." I was in machine repair, and I tried to get close to Ta Vet to attract him. Ta Vet and I had known one another since I was first at State Garments, but I did not yet know his heart, and did not dare attract him. Ta Vet had joined the revolution long ago, but from the time he had been a sewing machine repairman in the North until he had come to State Garments he had never been a group leader or team chairman like the others. Initially, I pretended to ask him if in the future our society might have salaries, coffee, and noodles. He said, "What hope is there? Since I joined the revolution in the North until now, I have never been comfortable or eaten my fill." I asked him, "Brother, since you joined the revolution have you ever been a chairman like the others?" He said he had been only been a combatant up until then. I said, "Brother you have worked without any backing, so if you work until you die you will never be anything like the others. I don't know why you try so hard now. If you strive, who can you give it to? Do just enough." After I said that, he liked me very much and worked just to get it off his hands. Later on I reeducated him, "Brother, find backing, in case later you can become a group or team chairman like the others." He said, "I want to find a backer, but I don't know who to look to." I said, "Brother, follow me; I have backers in Brother Lon and Brother Hēng, and Brother Lon and Brother Hēng have very many forces, in cutting and folding, in lathes, in electro-plating, in buttons, in vehicles, in carpentry." Ta Vet said, "Brother, if you help me find backers, I will follow you in everything." I said, "Brother, if you come over to Brother Hēng and Brother Lon, you will have to do activities to destroy the revolution so this society will not prosper, and we will gather forces for upper echelon. When there are many of us, including the group and team and section chairmen and the ministry chairmen, we can do whatever we want. It won't be tense like it is now." He said, "Destroy how?" I said, "Brother, what is there to wonder about, if the technology depends on us. If we make the sewing machines sew, they sew. If we damage them, what is the difficulty?" He agreed with me, and I told him that we had to be vigilant, and not talk about anything breaking secrecy and leading to all our deaths. I reported to Brother Hēng, who told me, "Brother, instruct Ta Vet to do continuous activities with the sewing machines." After I attracted him, Ta Vet and I conducted activities in sewing machine repair, causing the machines given to them to break needles by putting the needles out of balance with the bobbin-keepers, causing the stitches to jump by loosening the thread tension, causing the machines to frequently break down. Sometimes in one day a machine would be blocked four to ten times and could not sew. These activities have been constant until now, and Ta Vet still was active like this, one time breaking thread, and the next time breaking needles, or causing the stitches to be uneven, and throwing away a number of bobbins and spools.

During approximately late 77 or early 78, Brother Yong had me go back to vehicles. During early 78, I don't remember during which month, Brother Hēng called me and Comrades Hoeun, Loeum, Thân, Lon, Hat, Ta Y, and Ngoeun to a meeting in a house in front of the garage again. Then Brother Hēng said, "According to what Brother Yong told me, our forces are almost everywhere in Phnom Penh, in the ministries, in the Zones, and Brother Yong has had me call all you comrades to this meeting today so we can all know that in April at the Independence celebration, our forces have prepared a plan to prepare forces to make a coup throughout the country, in Phnom Penh as well as in the Zones, including the military too. At Angkar's location, Brother Pâng is leading it, to overthrow the Communist Party of Kampuchea. In particular, in our ministry where Brother Yong personally will lead, and according to his instructions, our location must rise up and overtly oppose with them to create confusion throughout Phnom Penh. Our ministry will act along the women's spearheads with Sister Von leading. Those of us in the Youth [Yuvoan] must all act with Brother Yong in the lead, since Comrade Lon has been arrested by Angkar already. But now, we must first build many forces. After that, we must incite the masses to be complicated, stir them up to demand setting up families, incite them about the bad food, and wait for Brother Yong to conduct activities and not resolve what the masses demand and make them complicated. When the coup occurs, we will all rise up together. After we win, it will certainly be comfortable, and we will all become senior people." After receiving these plans, Hat and I contacted Long, Hoeun, Loeum, Noeun, Ta Y, and Ngoeun, to stir them up by saying, "Look. Angkar said that it would arrange wives for youth 25 years of age. Now our 25-year-old comrades still have not had wives arranged for them. How can we create from 16 to 60 million people by acting like that? If we want to quickly reach that, we must propose them everywhere. If not, they'll be 30 years old and still not have them." After stirring things up, our comrades everywhere asked for marriage partners. When Brother Yong acted by saying no, our comrades went around complaining about their requests for marriage having been refused. Also, we incited by saying, "Angkar says that there are equal rights, but in fact the cadres can move about as they please, and when the masses ask to go visit relatives or to go look for a little something outside the ministry, they can't. Whether during work time or rest time, they can't go. How is that equality?" Then Hat and I built one force in driving, Comrade Hâm, a combatant, originally from the North. Hâm was skillful at going around complaining about Angkar seldom arranging marriages and complaining about not getting to eat his fill. In early 78, I, Hat, Long, Hoeun, Loeum, Noeun, Ta Y, Ngoeun, Nhăm met together during rest periods, at meals, and in the evenings, and we thought that we would clearly win over the Communist Party of Kampuchea.

In about early April 78, Brother Hēng called me, Hat, Hoeun, Noeun, Ta Y, and Long to another meeting at the same house. At first, Brother Hēng had each section report how they had acted to build forces. Long reported that he had built two forces, combatants in the electro-plating team, Hean and Vun, from the North. Noeun reported that he had not yet built any forces, and just only carried out activities to stir up opposition to the [Party] line. Hoeun reported that he had built two forces, combatants in lathes, one named Phâl, one named Boeun. Phâl was from the North. Boeun came from the East. Ta Y reported that he and Comrade Ngoeun had not yet built any forces, but he had carried out destructive activities. Hat reported on activities like those I have reported to Angkar above. After the reports were finished, Hēng instructed us to strive to gather up more forces. When we had many forces, we would certainly win. Another thing, we had to ready forces to make it easy when the coup came.

Later on, Angkar arrested Comrade Von (female). Then Brother Hēng too was arrested and disappeared. The Angkar moved a number of forces from Kâ 4 to come to State Garments. Still later on, Comrade Hoeun met Hat and me near the lathe building. Hoeun said that we should not yet lose hope. Brother Hēng and Brother Von were gone, but there was still Brother Yong, and Brother Yong had instructed us to postpone activities and not yet do anything strong because Angkar was monitoring us. If we act in small scale, don't let them take notice. Now Brother Yong has taken two more of his forces from Kâ 4. Hat asked their names. Hoeun told me and Hat that one was Comrade Choeun and one was Comrade Hoeun, and that they were are at folding and cutting. (Choeun is now a company chairman in the Youth at State Garments. Hoeun is now a deputy company chairman in the Youth at State Garments. The pasts of Choeun and Hoeun are unknown. I do know that they came from Office Kâ 4.) Later, Hat and I and Comrade Hiem were active spilling oil, wasting files and saws, throwing them away after little use, throwing keys in the sand, and we continued constant incitement activities opposing the Party line. In approximately June or July 78, Brother Yong too was arrested by Angkar. My people became more frightened because we had lost our backer from above; Brother Lin at Angkar's location frequently came down to the State Garment Ministry.

In August 78, Brother Lin came down to set up the appointment of the new State Garment Ministry secretary, who was from Srè Âmbel. After the ministry committee was set up, he organized the Youth into platoons and companies, and he selected Comrade Choeun as chairman and Comrade Hoeun as deputy chairman of the Youth Company. He had me be Member of the Company [Committee]. When this was set up, our forces had control of the 1st Platoon as well; Comrade Chhăm from the fishery site of the State Garment Ministry was in charge as chairman, and Comrade Noeun in buttons came to take charge as deputy platoon chairman. Comrade Chhun came from the fishery along with Comrade Chhăm as well, to be the member of the platoon [committee].

About ten days after the company was set up, while coming from dinner, I sat and talked with Comrade Hoeun, the company deputy from Office Kôr 9, about a wife, about having me help and seeing if she was pretty or not, since Hoeun had requested a wife. After talking with Hoeun, I asked Hoeun, "Hoeun, I heard from Hoeun at lathes that you were one of Brother Yong's forces from Office Kâ 4, is that right?" Hoeun seemed both to want to tell me and not want to tell me. I said, "Don't hide anything; I am also one of Yong's forces." Hoeun said, "I have indeed been one of Brother Yong's forces since I was at Kâ 4." I asked who had come with him from Kâ 4. Hoeun told me, "Brother Choeun was the force of Brother Yong who came with me to Garments. Hoeun said, "Uncle, if you know already, help in not telling anyone, be vigilant that Angkar does not learn of all of us." Houen asked me how many of Brother Yong's forces were left at this location, and I said that there were many. In vehicles, Comrades Hat, Hiem, Hâm; in carpentry, Comrade Nhăm, Chean; in lathes, Comrades Hoeun, Try, Phâl, Boeun, Thân, Pech, Thea; in buttons, Comrade Loeum; in electro-plating, Comrade Long, Hean, Vun; in folding and cutting, Comrades Ngoeun, Ta Y, Rēm; and the entire 1st Platoon Committee, Comrades Chhăm, Noeun, and Chhun. Comrade Noeun said, "Many of our forces remain, but now we had to postpone activities first, because Brother Lin is monitoring us. Wait for me to resolve this with Bother Choeun and see what to do." Later, probably in August 78, Comrade Hoeun called me to a house in front of Office Kôr 9. Choeun went too. Then Choeun asked about how many remaining forces there were in the State Garment Ministry. I told Choeun what the same thing I had reported to Comrade Hoeun before. Comrade Hoeun said, "The situation now is not good. After the arrest of Brother Yong, Brother Lin monitored us, if in this situation we continue activities it certainly will be dangerous and none of us will be left. We have not yet grasped the new ministry secretary either. So, Uncles Mey and Hoeun must tell out forces in each section to postpone activities for a while, because the situation is not yet quiet, and our backers are gone too. Until we can grasp the situation, wait and think about this further." The next day I met Brothers Hoeun and Noeun at the lathe site, and I told Hoeun and Noeun what Comrade Choeun had instructed. I said, "Choeun has instructed me to have our people postpone activities the situation is not good, especially in lathes, where they have been quick to take the most notice, because we have no strong backing. So Houen has told our people to postpone activities. After meeting Hoeun and Noeun, I went to tell Comrades Hiem and Hat at the vehicle location. Hoeun went to tell Comrade Ngoeun and Ta Y and the folding and cutting location. I went to tell Hat, Hiem, Nhăm, and Chean, and I went to the plating site to meet Comrades Long and Loeum. I called Long and Loeum to tell them at the location where Long was resting, the same as I had told Hoeun and Noeun. The next day, I met Comrades Chhăm and Chhun at the new kitchen location. I called Chhăm and Chhun to a location west of the kitchen, and told them, "Comrade Choeun told me to come and tell you to postpone activities for a while, because we already know the current situation, we have lost our backing too, and Brother Lin is monitoring us. Wait until he tells us to act before doing anything else."

In approximately early September 78, Comrade Choeun had me and Hoeun call and tell Comrades Chhăm, Noeun, Long, Loeum, Ta Y, Ngoeun, and Hoeun to come to a meeting on 7 September at the house in front of the Phsar Au Russei market at 7 at night. I went to tell Comrades Chhăm, Chhun, Noeun, Houen, Hat, and Long. Comrade Hoeun went to tell Ta Y and Comrade Ngoeun what Comrade Choeun had said. On the night of 7 September 78, we met in the house in front of the garage. We had met in that house in company meetings with our comrades, and they did not notice. At first, Comrade Choeun said, "The situation now in our ministry had improved, since Brother Lin does not come much, and Brother Văn, the new ministry secretary has no grasp on us. Now what do we do?" Our people in the sections said it was up to Brother. Comrade Choeun said, "We must continue on, with me as the protector. In doing this, we must know how to survey the situation to see what we can do. Don't force it, in buttons, in lathes, in plating, folding and cutting, carpentry and vehicles and in sewing machines, the most important thing is to destroy. First, stir up opposition to the Party line. As for building forces, postpone that, it cannot yet be done because the masses understand the line and they monitor us. Our direction of action is to destroy the materials used for work as we have been doing, and to impede at the same time. Second, in the ministry today, aside from Garments, we are making a new kitchen, digging ponds to raise fish, and arranging marriages for our comrades. In this work, Uncles Mey and Hoeun are already in charge and must work in these spearheads to impede, to make the masses complicated. Third, in the ministry today, we see that we have not resolved livelihood in food and vegetables. There are pigs and cattle, but Angkar had proposed saving the pigs for visitors, and lets us slaughter one cow per month. Therefore, in each section we must use this matter to stir up things, saying that the new ministry committee does not know how to solve the livelihood of the masses and leaves the masses to eat fermented fish and fish sauce, and one dish of soup, and say that the new ministry committee does not know how to lead the masses, and every day thinks just of playing around and is useless. Stir things up however you can so the masses are in conflict and lose faith in the new ministry committee. When they are in conflict, the ministry's work will be impeded and not advance, and we can gather up many forces without difficulty." After the meeting, Comrades Chhăm, Chhun, and Noeun who were building the new kitchen began a slow-down, not being on the offensive, letting anyone who worked go ahead and work, and letting anyone who walked around and did little work just walk around. They reported upward that they were short of bricks, short of sand, had no trucks for transport, and had no truck permits. There were trucks, but Choeun did not arrange them in time, and let Comrade Hiem conduct vehicular activities by not making deliveries in a timely way, transporting one load instead of two. Hoeun and I acted to arrange marriages for our comrades. The Party designated 23 years old and up for male youths. I arranged for some 22 years olds, but not for some 23 years olds, telling them that the Party had not yet made a decision, causing our comrades to be in ideological conflict with the new ministry committee and to not work hard. In digging the ponds, the ministry had me accept a month long plan. I delayed, not solving things in a timely way, and when it rained did not arrange to take along water pumps to pump so the digging could continue, taking two or three days to solve. During September 78, when Hoeun was in lathes, he went to set up sewing machine forces. According to what Hoeun told me, he and Ta Vet damaged some sewing machines by leaving them in the warehouse when it flooded and they were all ruined.

In early October, my group began inciting opposition to the Party at the State Garment Ministry. At meal time, I, Long, Hoeun, Ta Y, Comrades Ngoeun, Chhăm, Chhun, Noeun, Hat, Hiem, and Loeum walked around saying that the Party had set the goal of solving the livelihood of the masses regularly having two dishes per meal, so now, when there were cattle and pigs, they did not allow them to be slaughtered, but left us to eat fermented fish and fish sauce. If the ministry committee would not resolve this, then who would have the strength to work? And the ministry committee never did anything, just thought about playing every day going back and forth, so what could be done so upper echelon Angkar would learn of this and resolve it? After stirring this up, some of our comrades who believed the incitement walked around talking with one another. Then Comrade Hoeun, the deputy company chairman, told Chhăm that we should do whatever necessary to create turmoil. Then Comrades Chhăm and Chhun killed a dog, and Comrades Chean and Nhăm also killed a dog for our comrades to eat, when someone asked they said that there was too little food and no one solved it, so this had to be done to get something to eat.

On 8 October, Choeun had me and Comrade Hoeun go to call Comrades Long, Hoeun, Chhăm, Chhun, Noeun, Loeum, Ta Y, Ta Vet, Ngoeun, and Hat to a meeting at the same location at 7 in the evening. When we met, Choeun said, "In the past, we have carried out activities well and secrecy had not been broken either, because I helped to protect you constantly. Now is a good opportunity for us to continue. We have already grasped the direction of the Party to have the ministry go on an offensive to make garments to send to the various Zones by the end of this year. Also, we have heard the radio broadcast that the Yuon are preparing to attack Kampuchea during this upcoming dry season. At that time the Party will just think about the Yuon attacking, and will not think about us. We will have time to act to make internal confusion. Our direction is to do whatever necessary at year end to impede work in the ministry so it will not succeed according the Party's plans, to obstruct work in the ministry until we in each section can do destructive activities in the sections to obstruct both garment making and repairing sewing machined to supply to the Zones. Another destructive activity was to destroy the fabric warehouse. If we were to burn it down, that would quickly break secrecy, since they were monitoring, and not a lot would burn because the water trucks were constantly on duty as well. Now we have just Comrade Hoeun, the deputy company [chairman] in charge of the warehouse. We must take acid from Comrade Hoeun's site so Ta Y can sneak and pour it on the cloth. After a long time it will all go bad, and they will not notice it. And the incitement of confusion, having the masses demand two dishes at each meal and attacking the ministry committee must continue too. The important thing is to attack Comrade Yoeun, the ministry deputy chairman, first because Comrade Yoeun has many weak points that Brother Văn, and second he does not well understand the theory of reeducating our comrades. He is extravagant, from wearing watches to changing his clothing constantly; he does not have many old things. If the masses lose faith, he will certainly fall. If Comrade Yoeun falls, we must stick close to Brother Văn, because Brother Văn likes me. If I am promoted to member or ministry deputy, we can act as we please without breaking secrecy, because I will have control of the situation, and will help protect constantly. After the meeting, I joined in activities with Comrade Hiem and Hat, breaking six spark plugs while taking them out, and the wasteful of destruction saws, files, bolts, and oil continued. We also continued activities inciting attacks on the ministry committee demanding the resolutions of two dishes at each meal, but the importantly, the attacks on Comrade Yoeun saying first that Comrade Yoeun did not do anything other than constantly walk around every day showing off and changing his watches, clothing, and scarves, while the masses ate just fish sauce and fermented fish, and that was inappropriate. The following day I went to the construction site for the new kitchen. I called Chhăm outside, and asked Comrade Chhăm if there was anything at that location to destroy. Comrade Chhăm there were just nails, saws, planes and hatchets. I asked what he had already done, and Chhăm said he had thrown out a package of nails, some saws, and some planes into the garbage pile outside the fence. I said, "Chhăm, whatever you, Noeun, and Chhun do, do it so they do not learn about it." The following day, Comrade Houen, the company [chairman] told me that he had carried out activities with Ta Y, Ngoeun, and Choeun, cutting garments leaving large scrap pieces and throwing them away, sewing slowly, sewing and breaking many needles, and throwing away thread. Hoeun said that Comrade Long had burned up a sewing machine drive wheel and had held tension take-ups and burned up the take-ups in a number of other sewing machines. I asked Hoeun about the destruction of the cloth in the warehouse by putting acid on it, about whether or not he had already done that. Hoeun said that he had not yet been able to do it, because the situation had not yet been favorable. Later, on 28 October 78, I was arrested by Angkar.

6 November 1978
Person confessing [Thumbprint]
[Signature]
Chum Manh alias Mey

Interrogation Office
[Signature]
Sēng

LIST OF FORCES INVOLVED IN THE HISTORY

1	Tek	Former timber and soil transport business owner [thăokè] in Phnom Penh. Present unknown.
2	Tĭt	Former truck boss of Thăokè Tek. Born in Lôp Pha-ie. Present unknown.
3	Hĕng	Corporal looking after the trucks of Thăokè Tek. Present unknown.
4	Huon	Former cyclo worker in Phnom Penh. Separated from one another on 17 April. Present unknown.
5	Phy	Former cyclo worker in Phnom Penh. Present unknown.
6	Thoeun	Former cyclo worker in Phnom Penh. Present unknown.
7	Vĭn	Former cyclo worker in Phnom Penh. Present unknown.
8	Hoeun	Ice seller at Tuol Kouk Market. Present unknown.
9	Chân	Former cyclo worker in Phnom Penh. Present unknown.
10	Yun	Truck boss for Thăokè Tek. Present unknown.
11	Choeun	Truck boss for Thăokè Tek. Present unknown.
12	Thân	Forestry boss at Kratie. Present unknown.
13	Chhorn	Forestry boss at Kratie. Present unknown.
14	Khân	Forestry boss at Kratie. Present unknown.
15	Chèm	Former cyclo worker in Phnom Penh. Present unknown.
16	Vân	Former cyclo worker in Phnom Penh. Present unknown.
17	Chhĕng	Former cyclo worker in Phnom Penh. Present unknown.
18	Mân	Former cyclo worker in Phnom Penh. Present unknown.
19	Oeun	Taxi boss at Phsar Thmei. Present unknown.
20	Phĕng	Taxi boss at Phsar Thmei. Present unknown.
21	Huon	Taxi boss at Phsar Thmei. Present unknown.
22	Sreu	Chairman, Office 11, Water Transport. Now arrested.
23	Chhăm	Chairman of small motor boat team, Office 11. Now arrested.

24	Phat	Chairman of small motor boat team, Office 11. Now arrested.
25	Èk	Old worker. In 75 was still repairing small motor boats at Office 11. Present unknown, because I was separated from him in 75.
26	Sâm	Old worker. In 75 was still repairing small motor boats at Office 11. Present unknown.
27	Suon	Old worker. In 75 was still repairing small motor boats at Office 11. Present unknown.
28	Mân	Secretary of the Water Transport Ministry. Now arrested and disappeared.
29	Kun	Secretary of the State Garment Ministry. Now arrested.
30	Khân (female)	Secretary of the State Garment Ministry. Now arrested.
31	Von (female)	Secretary of the State Garment Ministry. Arrested and disappeared.
32	Yong	Secretary of the State Garment Ministry. Arrested and disappeared.
33	Lon	In charge of [Male] Youth at State Garments. Arrested and disappeared.
34	Chhum	Chairman, Office Kôr 9, State Garments. Arrested and disappeared.
35	Saut	Lathe Shop Chairman, State Garments. Arrested.
36	Răn	Cambodian medicine medic, State Garments. Arrested and disappeared.
37	Phăn	Construction Chairman, State Garments. Arrested and disappeared.
38	Săo	Past unknown. From the North. In 76, in charge of vehicles at State Garments. Now at State Warehouse. Job unknown, I never met him after 77.
39	Hat	Carpentry and vehicle team and chairman at state Garments. Arrested.
40	Hoeun	Past unknown. From the North. Now in charge of sewing machine warehouse at State Garments.
41	Try	Deputy of the lathe team [chairman] at State Garments. Arrested and brought in along with me.

42	Thân	Past unknown. From the North. In 77, lathe team chairman at State Garments. Now a combatant.
43	Thol	Combatant at the lathe shop at state sewing. Arrested.
44	Hiem	Past unknown. From the North. Now a deputy vehicle team chairman at State Garments.
45	Srâs	Combatant, driver, State Garments. Arrested and disappeared.
46	Hēng	Chairman, vehicles and carpenters, State Garments. Arrested and disappeared.
47	Ta Y	A sewing machine repairman from the Old Society [Sihanouk Era], but I don't know the location. From the North. Now a cutting and folding team chairman at State Garments.
48	Ngoeun	Past unknown. From the North. Now a team folding/cutting team chairman at State Garments.
49	Chean	Past unknown. From the North. Now a combatant carpenter at State Garments.
50	Nhăm	Past unknown. From the North. Now a team member in carpentry at State Garments.
51	Chhun	Past unknown. From the North. Now a Member, 1st Platoon, State Garments.
52	Loeum	Past unknown. From the North. Now chairman of a button making team at State Garments.
53	Chhăm	Past unknown. From the North. Now chairman of 1st Platoon, State Garments.
54	Noeun	Past unknown. From the North. Now deputy chairman of 1st Platoon, State Garments.
55	Long	Past unknown. From the North. Now team chairman in electroplating at State Garments.
56	Phăt (female)	The wife of Lon, in charge of the garment warehouse, State Garments Ministry. Now arrested and disappeared.
57	Ta Vet	A former sewing machine repairman from the Old Society. From the North. Now a combatant in sewing machine repair at State Garments.

58	Hâm	Former rice farmer. From the North. Now a combatant and driver at State Garments.
59	Phâl	Past unknown. From the North. Now a combatant at the lathe shop at State Garments.
60	Boeun	Past unknown. From the East. Now a combatant at the lathe shop at State Garments.
61	Hean	Past unknown. From the North. Now a combatant in electroplating at State Garments.
62	Vun	Past unknown. From the North. Now a combatant in electroplating at State Garments.
63	Pech	Past unknown. From the North. Now a team chairman in lathes at State Garments.
64	Thea	Former rice farmer. From the North. Now a combatant in lathes at State Garments
65	Rēt	Past unknown. From the North. Now a combatant in folding and cutting at State Garments.
66	Choeun	I have no clear grasp on his past. According to what Choeun told me, he was from Preah Vihear. Now a company chairman at State Garments. Before coming to Garments, was at Office Kâ 4 with Yong.
67	Hoeun	Past unknown. Before coming to State Garments, was at Office Kâ 4 with Yong and Choeun. Now a deputy company chairman at State Garments.
68	Pâng	The Ministry S.71 Secretary. Arrested and disappeared.

End of confession.

Chum Mey at the Khmer Rouge Tribunal. Photo by Heng Sinith.

The Victim was Arrested in 1977

Interrogation Room

They have walked me to ask the questions.